celebrating
COOKIES
book 2

LEISURE ARTS, INC.
Little Rock, Arkansas

EDITORIAL STAFF

Editor in Chief Susan White Sullivan
Designer Relations Director Debra Nettles
Special Projects Director Susan Frantz Wiles
Craft Publications Director Cheryl Johnson
Foods Editor Jane Kenner Prather
Contributing Test Kitchen Staff Nora Faye
  Spencer Clift, Celia Berry Martin, Jennifer Boyle
  Newsome, Norma Lee Tober, and Teresa Trainor
Editorial Writer Susan McManus Johnson
Senior Prepress Director Mark Hawkins
Art Publications Director Rhonda Shelby
Contributing Artist Horizon Design, LLC
Art Category Manager Lora Puls
Graphic Artists Janie Wright, Becca Snider, and
  Dana Vaughn
Imaging Technicians Stephanie Johnson and
  Mark R. Potter
Photography Director Katherine Laughlin
Contributing Photographers Mark Mathews and
  Ken West
Contributing Photo Stylist Christy Myers
Publishing Systems Administrator Becky Riddle
Publishing Systems Assistants Clint Hanson and
  Keiji Yumoto
Mac Information Technology Specialist
  Robert Young

BUSINESS STAFF

Vice President and Chief Operations Officer
  Tom Siebenmorgen
Director of Finance and Administration
  Laticia Mull Dittrich
Vice President, Sales and Marketing
  Pam Stebbins
Sales Director Martha Adams
Marketing Director Margaret Reinold
Creative Services Director Jeff Curtis
Information Technology Director
  Hermine Linz
Controller Francis Caple
Vice President, Operations Jim Dittrich
Comptroller, Operations Rob Thieme
Retail Customer Service Manager Stan Raynor
Print Production Manager Fred F. Pruss

Library of Congress Control Number: 2009930564
ISBN-13: 978-1-60900-006-6

contents

CELEBRATING COOKIES

Cookie lovers, get ready to celebrate!
This encore cookbook has more of that unforgettable,
melt-in-your-mouth goodness you crave. With appetizing,
up-close photos of all 75 recipes, this fresh batch
of our very best cookies includes a wide variety
to please everyone in the family. You'll find irresistible
cookie-jar classics, playful snacks for children,
fun treats for lots of holidays and special occasions,
and elegant cookies with sophisticated flavors.
Let the party begin!

SUCCESS WITH COOKIES

You can be most successful at baking cookies when you know
a few tips from the pros. Here are some of our favorites.

BAKING TIPS

- To keep dough from sticking to cookie cutters, dip in flour before cutting out each cookie. Metal cookie cutters with a good edge usually will cut better than plastic cutters.
- When you need to drizzle a small amount of icing or melted chocolate and you do not have a pastry or decorating bag, use a resealable plastic bag. After filling bag half full of icing or chocolate, seal the bag and cut off a small tip of one corner. Make your first snip small, as you can always cut off more if needed.
- When softening butter in the microwave, be careful not to let it melt, as melted butter results in a flatter cookie.
- Bake one batch of cookies at a time on the center rack of a preheated oven. If baking two batches at a time, space evenly for good air circulation.
- Oven temperatures vary, so always check cookies 1 minute before the earliest time stated in recipe to prevent overbaking.

SUPPLIES

- Use heavy-gauge, shiny aluminum sheets with low or no sides for even browning of cookies. Dark coating on sheets will affect browning. Insulated sheets may make it more difficult to determine doneness; also, cookies with a high butter content will spread out before the shape is set.
- Using parchment paper eliminates the need to grease cookie sheets and makes cleanup easy.

STORAGE TIPS

- After completely cooling cookies, store each kind separately to prevent flavors from blending. Soft cookies will cause crisp cookies to become soft.
- Store soft cookies in an airtight container. Use waxed paper between layers to prevent cookies from sticking together.
- Store crisp cookies in a tin or container with a loose-fitting lid. In humid areas, the lid will need to be tighter so cookies will stay crisp.
- Store bar cookies in the pan covered with foil or remove from pan and store in an airtight container.
- If soft cookies have dried out, place a slice of apple or bread with cookies for a few days in an airtight container.
- Most cookies (except meringues) can be frozen up to six months. Freeze in plastic freezer bags or plastic containers with tight-fitting lids.

MAILING TIPS

- Soft, moist cookies and bar cookies are suitable for mailing. Line a sturdy box with waxed paper, aluminum foil, or plastic wrap. Place a layer of crumpled waxed paper or paper towels in bottom of box. Depending on type of cookie, wrap back-to-back if they are flat, in small groups in plastic bags, or individually.
- Pack crumpled waxed paper or paper towels snugly between cookies to prevent them from shifting. Tape box securely closed.

FAVORITES

There are two kinds of cookie fanatics:
those who insist on a single favorite and those
who celebrate all the different kinds of cookies.
This collection has best-loved recipes to please all of you.

Tart, sweet Lemon Bars are always in demand when refreshments are served at popular social gatherings. A drizzling of lemony icing makes these extra good.

lemon bars

In a medium bowl, combine 2 cups flour and ½ cup confectioners sugar. Stir in melted butter, mixing well. Spread mixture in a greased 9 x 13 x 2-inch baking pan. Bake at 350° for 20 to 25 minutes.

In a medium bowl, beat granulated sugar and eggs together until fluffy. In a small bowl, combine baking powder and remaining ¼ cup flour; add to sugar mixture. Stir in 2 cups coconut and ¼ cup lemon juice. Pour over baked crust. Return to oven and bake at 350° for 25 more minutes or until top is lightly browned; cool.

In a small bowl, combine remaining 1 cup confectioners sugar and remaining 1 to 2 tablespoons lemon juice; drizzle over baked mixture. Sprinkle with remaining ½ cup coconut. Cut into 2-inch squares.

YIELD: about 2 dozen bars

2¼ **cups all-purpose flour, divided**

1½ **cups confectioners sugar, divided**

1 **cup butter or margarine, melted**

2 **cups granulated sugar**

4 **eggs**

1 **teaspoon baking powder**

2½ **cups sweetened shredded coconut, divided**

¼ **cup plus 1 to 2 tablespoons lemon juice, divided**

Great energy boosters when you're on the go, Trail Cookies are packed with pecans, oats, and wheat germ; raisins and coconut make them naturally sweet and chewy. When it's time to relax, nutty Chunky Chocolate Cookies are a good choice.

chunky chocolate cookies

In a large bowl, cream butter and sugars until fluffy. Add egg and vanilla; beat until smooth. In a small bowl, combine flour, cocoa, baking powder, baking soda, and salt. Add dry ingredients to creamed mixture; stir until a soft dough forms. Stir in chocolate chunks and pecans.

Drop tablespoonfuls of dough 2 inches apart onto an ungreased baking sheet. Bake at 375° for 6 to 8 minutes or until cookies are set and bottoms are lightly browned. Transfer cookies to a wire rack to cool.

YIELD: about 4$\frac{1}{2}$ dozen cookies

- 1 cup butter or margarine, softened
- $\frac{3}{4}$ cup firmly packed brown sugar
- $\frac{1}{2}$ cup granulated sugar
- 1 egg
- 1 teaspoon vanilla extract
- 1$\frac{3}{4}$ cups all-purpose flour
- $\frac{1}{4}$ cup cocoa
- $\frac{1}{2}$ teaspoon baking powder
- $\frac{1}{2}$ teaspoon baking soda
- $\frac{1}{2}$ teaspoon salt
- 1 package (10 ounces) milk chocolate chunks
- $\frac{1}{2}$ cup chopped pecans

trail cookies

In a large bowl, cream butter and sugars until fluffy. Add egg and vanilla; beat until smooth. In a small bowl, combine flour, wheat germ, and baking powder. Add dry ingredients to creamed mixture; stir until a soft dough forms. Stir in raisins, pecans, coconut, and oats.

Drop heaping tablespoonfuls of dough 2 inches apart onto a greased baking sheet. Bake at 350° for 11 to 13 minutes or until edges are lightly browned. Cool cookies on baking sheet 5 minutes; transfer to a wire rack to cool completely.

YIELD: about 2$\frac{1}{2}$ dozen cookies

- $\frac{1}{2}$ cup butter or margarine, softened
- $\frac{1}{2}$ cup firmly packed brown sugar
- $\frac{1}{2}$ cup granulated sugar
- 1 egg
- 1 teaspoon vanilla extract
- $\frac{3}{4}$ cup all-purpose flour
- $\frac{3}{4}$ cup wheat germ
- 1 teaspoon baking powder
- 1 cup raisins
- $\frac{1}{2}$ cup chopped pecans
- $\frac{1}{3}$ cup sweetened shredded coconut
- $\frac{1}{3}$ cup old-fashioned oats

Cute as a button—and delicious, too! These luscious snacks combine two of our favorite flavors. The creamy peanut butter filling is piped to perfection using a decorating bag.

peanut butter-filled chocolate buttons

In a large bowl, cream butter and sugar until fluffy. Add egg, milk, and vanilla; beat until smooth. In a medium bowl, combine flour, cocoa, baking powder, and baking soda. Add dry ingredients to creamed mixture; stir until a soft dough forms. Cover and chill 2 hours or until dough is firm enough to handle.

Shape dough into 1-inch balls and place 1 inch apart on an ungreased baking sheet. Use finger or the back of a small, round measuring spoon to make an indentation in each ball. Spoon peanut butter into a decorating bag fitted with a large round tip (#11). Pipe a small amount of peanut butter into center of each ball. Bake at 350° for 6 to 8 minutes or until bottoms are browned. Cool cookies on baking sheet 3 minutes; transfer to a wire rack to cool completely. Store in single layers between sheets of waxed paper.

YIELD: about 7$\frac{1}{2}$ dozen cookies

1 cup butter or margarine, softened

1 cup sugar

1 egg

2 tablespoons milk

1 teaspoon vanilla extract

2$\frac{1}{2}$ cups all-purpose flour

$\frac{1}{2}$ cup cocoa

$\frac{3}{4}$ teaspoon baking powder

$\frac{1}{4}$ teaspoon baking soda

$\frac{3}{4}$ cup smooth peanut butter

These cookies will perk up your day, especially when you enjoy them with a fresh cup of coffee. Semisweet chocolate and instant coffee combine with the subtle flavor of almonds to give the cookies their rich charm.

mocha-almond cookies

In a large bowl, cream butter and brown sugar until fluffy. Add eggs and almond extract; beat until smooth. In a small bowl, combine flour, coffee granules, baking soda, and salt. Add dry ingredients to creamed mixture; stir until a soft dough forms. Stir in chocolate chips and almonds.

Drop tablespoonfuls of dough 2 inches apart onto a lightly greased baking sheet. Bake at 350° for 9 to 12 minutes or until edges are lightly browned. Transfer cookies to a wire rack to cool.

YIELD: about 3 dozen cookies

1 cup butter or margarine, softened

1 cup firmly packed brown sugar

2 eggs

1 teaspoon almond extract

2 cups all-purpose flour

2 tablespoons instant coffee granules

$1/2$ teaspoon baking soda

$1/4$ teaspoon salt

1 package (6 ounces) semisweet chocolate chips

$3/4$ cup sliced almonds, toasted and coarsely chopped

Flavored with ground pecans and freshly grated orange zest, this tender shortbread is the ultimate reward. Take a break and treat yourself!

orange-nut shortbread

Line a 9-inch square baking pan with aluminum foil, extending foil over opposite sides of pan; grease foil. Set aside.

In a medium bowl, cream butter, sugar, orange zest, and orange extract until fluffy. In a small bowl, combine flour and cornstarch. Add dry ingredients to creamed mixture; stir until a soft dough forms. Stir in ground pecans. Press dough into bottom of prepared pan. Sprinkle chopped pecans on top and lightly press into dough. Bake at 350° for 45 to 50 minutes or until golden in color.

Use ends of foil to immediately lift shortbread from pan. Cut warm shortbread into 2-inch squares; cool completely.

YIELD: about 16 squares

$3/4$ cup butter or margarine, softened

$1/2$ cup sugar

2 teaspoons grated orange zest

$1/2$ teaspoon orange extract

1 cup all-purpose flour

$1/2$ cup cornstarch

$1/2$ cup coarsely ground pecans

$1/4$ cup chopped pecans

Which do you want today: chocolate or vanilla? Why not enjoy both at once with these Two-Tone Cookies? The dark side is loaded with semisweet chocolate chips, and the light side is bursting with pecans. What a delicious flavor combination!

two-tone cookies

In a large bowl, cream butter and sugars until fluffy. Add eggs and vanilla; beat until smooth. In a small bowl, combine flour, baking soda, and salt. Add dry ingredients to creamed mixture; stir until a soft dough forms. Divide dough in half, adding melted chocolate and chocolate chips to half of dough. Add pecans to remaining half of dough.

Drop 1 tablespoonful of light dough onto a lightly greased baking sheet. Drop 1 tablespoonful of dark dough next to light dough with sides touching. Repeat with remaining dough, placing 2 inches apart. Bake at 350° for 6 to 8 minutes or until edges are lightly browned. Transfer cookies to a wire rack to cool.

YIELD: about 2 dozen cookies

$3/4$ cup butter or margarine, softened

$3/4$ cup granulated sugar

$3/4$ cup firmly packed brown sugar

2 eggs

2 teaspoons vanilla extract

$2^1/2$ cups all-purpose flour

1 teaspoon baking soda

$1/4$ teaspoon salt

3 ounces semisweet baking chocolate, melted and cooled

1 cup semisweet chocolate mini chips

1 cup chopped pecans, toasted

These moist treats should have been named Delicious Temptations! A brown sugar-oat mixture forms the crust and crumbled topping, while cherry pie filling and a sweetened cream cheese and pecan mixture are layered in between.

cherry-oat-nut squares

In a medium bowl, cream butter and brown sugar until fluffy. In a small bowl, combine oats, flour, baking soda, and salt. Add dry ingredients to creamed mixture; stir until well blended. Reserving $3/4$ cup oat mixture, firmly press remainder of mixture into bottom of a lightly greased 9 x 13-inch baking pan. Spread cherry pie filling over crust.

In a medium bowl, beat cream cheese and egg. Add confectioners sugar, vanilla, cinnamon, and nutmeg; beat until smooth. Stir in pecans. Spread cream cheese mixture over cherries. Crumble reserved oat mixture over cream cheese mixture. Bake at 350° for 40 to 45 minutes or until center is set and top is lightly browned. Cool in pan.

Cut into 2-inch squares. Store in refrigerator.

YIELD: about 2 dozen squares

$3/4$ cup butter or margarine, softened

1 cup firmly packed brown sugar

$1^1/2$ cups quick-cooking oats

$1^1/4$ cups all-purpose flour

$1/2$ teaspoon baking soda

$1/4$ teaspoon salt

1 can (21 ounces) cherry pie filling

1 package (3 ounces) cream cheese, softened

1 egg

$1^1/2$ cups confectioners sugar

1 teaspoon vanilla extract

$1/2$ teaspoon ground cinnamon

$1/8$ teaspoon ground nutmeg

1 cup finely chopped pecans, toasted

A sweet, mellow blending of butter and brown sugar makes Butterscotch Brownies stack up as an all-time favorite. Toasted pecans bring nutty texture to the moist bars.

butterscotch brownies

Line a 9 x 13-inch pan with aluminum foil, extending foil over ends of pan; grease foil. Set aside.

In a large bowl, cream butter and brown sugar until fluffy. Add eggs and vanilla; beat until smooth. In a small bowl, combine flour, baking powder, baking soda, and salt. Add dry ingredients to creamed mixture; stir until well blended. Stir in pecans.

Spread batter into prepared pan. Bake at 350° for 25 to 30 minutes or until brownies start to pull away from sides of pan. Cool in pan 15 minutes.

Use ends of foil to lift brownies from pan. Cut warm brownies into 2-inch squares.

YIELD: about 2 dozen brownies

$1/2$ cup butter or margarine, softened

2 cups firmly packed brown sugar

2 eggs

$1^1/2$ teaspoons vanilla extract

$1^3/4$ cups all-purpose flour

$1^1/2$ teaspoons baking powder

$1/2$ teaspoon baking soda

$1/4$ teaspoon salt

1 cup chopped pecans, toasted

Enticing flavors and nutty crunch make the world go round for cookie lovers! Hermits are chewy spice cookies that combine the goodness of raisins and walnuts with bold coffee and molasses. Cinnamon Bars keep it simple with a sprinkling of chopped pecans, and the recipe makes enough for a group.

cinnamon bars

Cream butter and sugar. Combine flour and cinnamon; gradually add to creamed mixture. Stir in egg yolk and vanilla until well blended.

Press dough into the bottom of a greased $10^1/_2$ x $15^1/_2$ x 1-inch-deep jellyroll pan. Brush egg white on top of dough. Sprinkle pecans over dough; press pecans into dough. Bake at 300° for 30 minutes. Cut into $1^1/_2$ x 3-inch bars while warm. Cool completely in pan.

YIELD: about 3 dozen bars

- 1 cup butter or margarine, softened
- $^3/_4$ cup sugar
- 2 cups all-purpose flour
- 3 teaspoons ground cinnamon
- 1 egg, separated
- 1 teaspoon vanilla extract
- 1 cup chopped pecans

hermits

In a large bowl, cream butter and brown sugar until fluffy. Add eggs, molasses, coffee, and vanilla; beat until smooth. In a medium bowl, combine flour, baking soda, baking powder, salt, and spices. Add dry ingredients to creamed mixture; stir until a soft dough forms. Stir in raisins and walnuts.

Drop tablespoonfuls of dough 2 inches apart onto a lightly greased baking sheet. Bake at 375° for 7 to 9 minutes or until tops are golden brown. Transfer cookies to a wire rack to cool.

YIELD: about 7 dozen cookies

- 1 cup butter or margarine, softened
- 2 cups firmly packed brown sugar
- 2 eggs
- $^1/_4$ cup molasses
- $^1/_4$ cup strongly brewed coffee, cooled
- 1 teaspoon vanilla extract
- 3 cups all-purpose flour
- 1 teaspoon baking soda
- 1 teaspoon baking powder
- 1 teaspoon salt
- 1 teaspoon ground cinnamon
- $^1/_2$ teaspoon ground allspice
- $^1/_4$ teaspoon ground nutmeg
- 2 cups golden raisins, coarsely chopped
- $1^1/_4$ cups chopped walnuts

Is it a cookie or a cake? Who wants to waste time arguing when there's a plate of these soft, chewy Fig Bars waiting? Just enjoy! You'll never go back to store-bought.

fig bars

For dough, cream butter and sugars in a large bowl until fluffy. Add honey, egg, and vanilla; beat until smooth. In a medium bowl, combine flours, baking soda, and salt. Add dry ingredients to creamed mixture; stir until a soft dough forms. Divide dough into fourths. Wrap in plastic wrap and chill 1 hour.

For filling, combine figs and water in a heavy medium saucepan over medium heat. Stirring constantly, bring mixture to a boil; boil 5 minutes. In a small bowl, combine sugar and flour; stir into fig mixture. Reduce heat to medium-low. Stirring frequently, cook mixture 10 minutes or until thickened. Remove from heat. Stir in walnuts and orange juice. Allow mixture to cool.

Between sheets of plastic wrap, roll out $1/4$ of dough at a time into an 8 x 12-inch rectangle. Remove top sheet of plastic wrap. Cut dough crosswise into four 3 x 8-inch pieces. Spread 2 tablespoons fig mixture down center of each length of dough. Slightly overlapping edges, fold long sides of each dough strip over filling in center. Using plastic wrap to lift dough, place dough strips, seam side down, 2 inches apart on an ungreased baking sheet. Remove plastic wrap. Bake at 350° for 11 to 13 minutes or until lightly browned. Cool cookies on baking sheet 5 minutes; transfer to a wire rack to cool completely. Cut into 2-inch-long bars.

YIELD: about 5 dozen bars

DOUGH

- $1/2$ cup butter or margarine, softened
- $1/2$ cup granulated sugar
- $1/2$ cup firmly packed brown sugar
- $1/3$ cup honey
- 1 egg
- 1 teaspoon vanilla extract
- $2 1/4$ cups all-purpose flour
- 1 cup whole-wheat flour
- $3/4$ teaspoon baking soda
- $1/2$ teaspoon salt

FILLING

- 2 cups finely chopped dried figs (about 8 ounces)
- $1 1/3$ cups water
- 1 cup sugar
- $1/4$ cup all-purpose flour
- $1/3$ cup chopped walnuts
- 3 tablespoons orange juice

Cookies so good, you'll think you're dreaming! These have a rich filling of sliced almonds, coconut, and chocolate chips spread over a buttery brown sugar crust.

chocolate-almond dream bars

Line a 9 x 13-inch baking pan with aluminum foil, extending foil over ends of pan; set aside.

For crust, mix flour, butter, and brown sugar in a medium bowl with a fork until well blended. Press crust into bottom of prepared pan. Bake at 350° for 10 minutes.

While crust is baking, combine almonds, coconut, chocolate chips, flour, baking powder, and salt in a medium bowl for filling. In a small bowl, beat brown sugar, eggs, and vanilla until well blended. Add to dry ingredients; stir until well blended. Spoon over hot crust. Bake at 350° for 15 to 20 more minutes or until center is set and top is lightly browned. Cool completely in pan.

Remove from pan using ends of foil. Cut into 1 x 2-inch bars.

YIELD: about 4 dozen bars

CRUST

- 1 cup all-purpose flour
- $1/2$ cup butter or margarine, softened
- $1/2$ cup firmly packed brown sugar

FILLING

- $1 1/4$ cups sliced almonds, toasted
- 1 cup sweetened shredded coconut
- $3/4$ cup semisweet chocolate chips
- 2 tablespoons all-purpose flour
- $3/4$ teaspoon baking powder
- $1/4$ teaspoon salt
- $3/4$ cup firmly packed brown sugar
- 2 eggs
- $1 1/2$ teaspoons vanilla extract

KIDS COLLECTION

If you want to make a child happy, baking homemade cookies is a good place to start. This collection of recipes is devoted to the familiar flavors and whimsical looks that kids love.

Crayons are at the heart of childhood's creative pleasures, and these colorful cookies are sure to multiply the fun! Beneath the brilliantly tinted icing are tender cookies flavored with corn flakes and peanut butter.

crayon cookies

For cookies, cream butter, shortening, and sugars in a large bowl until fluffy. Add peanut butter, eggs, and vanilla; beat until smooth. In a medium bowl, combine flour, crushed cereal, and salt. Add dry ingredients to creamed mixture; stir until a soft dough forms. Divide dough into fourths; wrap each fourth in plastic wrap. Chill 1 hour.

On a lightly floured surface, roll out $1/4$ of dough at a time into a 10-inch square. Cut out 1 x 5-inch cookies. Place on a greased baking sheet. Cut 1 end of each cookie to form a point; remove dough scraps. Bake at 350° for 8 to 10 minutes or until edges are lightly browned. Cool cookies on baking sheet 2 minutes; transfer to a wire rack to cool completely.

For icing, combine confectioners sugar and milk in a medium bowl. Transfer $1/2$ cup icing into each of 6 small bowls. Tint yellow, blue, red, orange, green, and black. Spoon icings into decorating bags fitted with small round tips. Outline and fill in "labels" with yellow, blue, red, orange, and green icing. Allow icing to harden.

Pipe names of colors and lines onto cookies with black icing. Allow icing to harden.

YIELD: about $6^1/2$ dozen cookies

COOKIES

- 1 cup butter or margarine, softened
- $1/2$ cup vegetable shortening
- $1^1/2$ cups granulated sugar
- $1/2$ cup firmly packed brown sugar
- 1 cup smooth peanut butter
- 2 eggs
- 1 teaspoon vanilla extract
- 4 cups all-purpose flour
- $1^1/4$ cups sweetened corn flake cereal, finely crushed
- $1/4$ teaspoon salt

ICING

- $7^1/2$ cups confectioners sugar
- 10 to 12 tablespoons milk
  - Yellow, blue, red, orange, green, and black paste food colorings

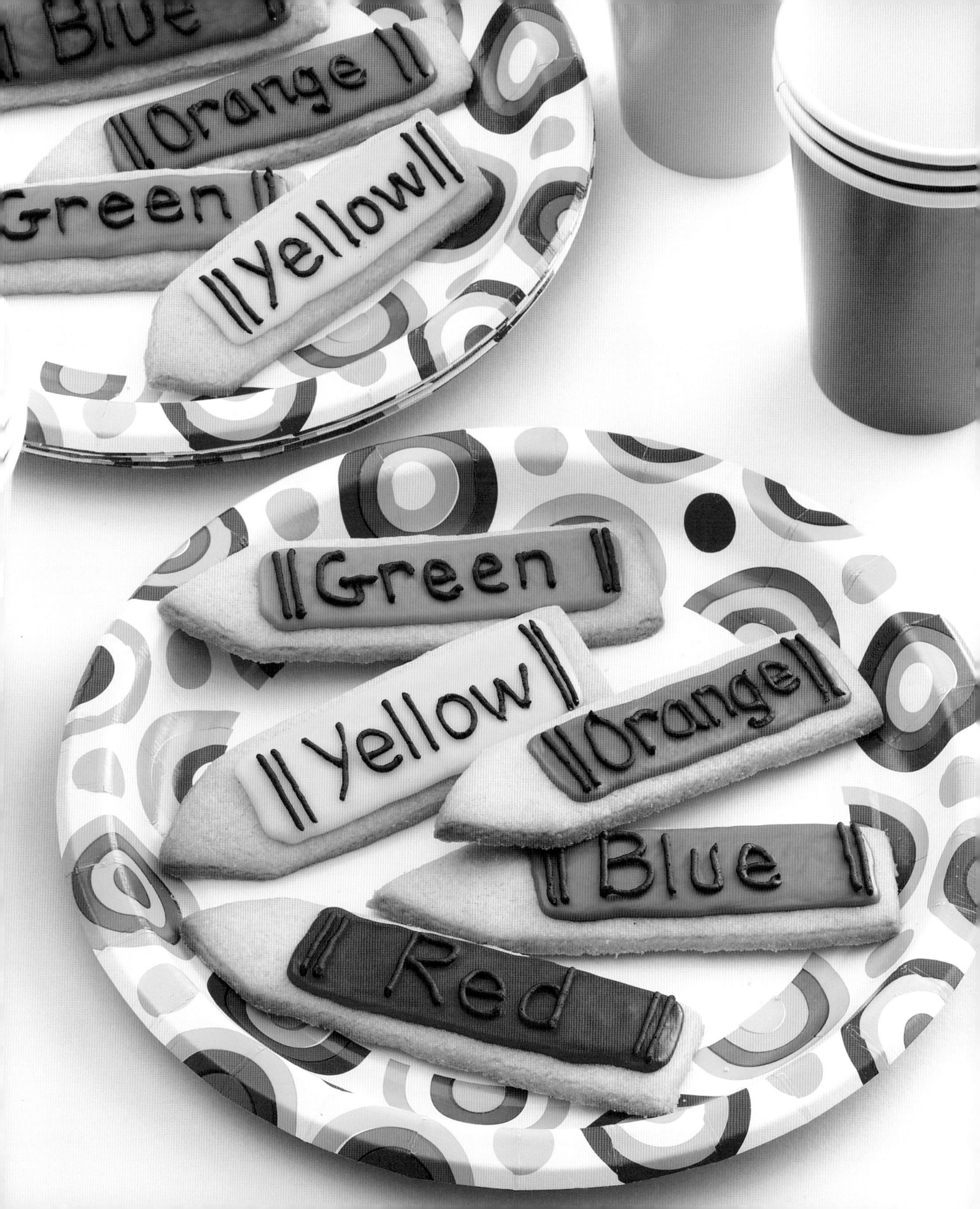
Blue
Orange
Green
Yellow
Green
Yellow
Orange
Blue
Red

Their name may be only half as silly as that of the traditional snickerdoodle cookie, but the cocoa makes this variation doubly good! The cracked texture and sugar-cinnamon coating will have kids reaching for these favorites again and again.

chocodoodles

In a large bowl, cream butter and 1½ cups sugar until fluffy. Add eggs and vanilla; beat until smooth. In a medium bowl, combine flour, cocoa, 1 teaspoon cinnamon, cream of tartar, baking soda, and salt. Add dry ingredients to creamed mixture; stir until a soft dough forms. In a small bowl, combine remaining 3 tablespoons sugar and 1¾ teaspoons cinnamon.

Shape dough into 1-inch balls and roll in sugar-cinnamon mixture. Place balls 2 inches apart on a lightly greased baking sheet. Bake at 375° for 6 to 8 minutes or until bottoms are lightly browned. Transfer cookies to a wire rack to cool.

YIELD: about 7 dozen cookies

1	cup butter or margarine, softened
1½	cups plus 3 tablespoons sugar, divided
2	eggs
1	teaspoon vanilla extract
2¼	cups all-purpose flour
½	cup cocoa
2¾	teaspoons ground cinnamon, divided
1	teaspoon cream of tartar
1	teaspoon baking soda
¼	teaspoon salt

When you bring out these UFO's (Undeniably Fun Objects), get ready for giggles that are out of this world! Accompany the delicious treats with Hairy Monsters, packed with peanuts and rolled in shredded coconut.

flying saucer cookies

Stirring constantly, melt candy coating in a small saucepan over low heat. Place each cookie on a fork and drip into candy coating until covered. Allow excess candy coating to drip back into pan.

Place cookies on a wire rack with waxed paper underneath. Before coating hardens, decorate with candies and pretzels to resemble flying saucers; allow coating to harden.

YIELD: 1 dozen cookies

12 ounces vanilla candy coating, chopped
1 dozen cookies (about 2½-inch diameter)
Variety of candies
Thin stick pretzels

hairy monsters

Whisking constantly, combine butter, sugar, and egg in a heavy medium skillet over medium heat. Add dates to butter mixture. Continue to cook and whisk mixture about 10 minutes, mashing as dates soften. Remove from heat; stir in cereal, peanuts, and vanilla.

When mixture is cool enough to handle, use greased hands to shape into 1-inch balls; roll in coconut. Cool.

YIELD: about 4 dozen cookies

½ cup butter or margarine
¾ cup sugar
1 egg
1 cup chopped dates
2 cups crispy rice cereal
1 cup coarsely chopped salted peanuts
1 teaspoon vanilla extract
1⅓ cups sweetened finely shredded coconut

Mama mia! This yummy pizza has a tender cookie crust and moist, rich toppings of coconut, pecans, and chocolate chips. This big creation is just right for parties.

cookie pizza

For crust, cream butter, shortening, and sugar in a large bowl until fluffy. Add egg and vanilla; beat until smooth. Stir in flour; knead until a soft dough forms. Press dough into bottom and up sides of a greased 12-inch round pizza pan.

For topping, sprinkle chocolate chips, pecans, and $\frac{1}{2}$ cup coconut evenly over crust. Pour condensed milk evenly over top. Bake at 350° for 25 to 30 minutes or until crust is golden brown. While cookie is still warm, place chocolate chunks on top and sprinkle with remaining $\frac{1}{4}$ cup coconut. Cool completely in pan.

YIELD: about 16 servings

CRUST

- $\frac{1}{4}$ cup butter or margarine, softened
- $\frac{1}{4}$ cup butter-flavored shortening
- $\frac{3}{4}$ cup firmly packed brown sugar
- 1 egg
- 1 teaspoon vanilla extract
- 1 cup all-purpose flour

TOPPING

- 1 cup (6 ounces) semisweet chocolate chips
- 1 cup finely chopped pecans
- $\frac{3}{4}$ cup sweetened shredded coconut, divided
- 1 can (14 ounces) sweetened condensed milk
- $\frac{1}{2}$ cup semi-sweet chocolate chunks

Ooey, gooey, and so good! You won't need a campfire to treat kids to the beloved taste of s'mores. These brownie-based goodies are baked in the oven, topped with graham cracker crumbs, chocolate chips, and miniature marshmallows.

s'more chocolate bars

In a large bowl, combine brownie mix, oil, water, and egg; stir until well blended. Pour into a greased 9 x 13-inch baking pan. Sprinkle graham cracker crumbs over batter. Bake at 350° for 20 minutes.

Sprinkle chocolate chips over brownies; top with marshmallows. Continue to bake at 350° for 8 to 10 more minutes or until marshmallows begin to brown. Cool in pan on a wire rack.

Use an oiled knife to cut into 1 x 2-inch bars.

YIELD: about 4 dozen bars

- 1 package (21.1 ounces) brownie mix
- $\frac{1}{2}$ cup vegetable oil
- $\frac{1}{2}$ cup water
- 1 egg
- 14 graham crackers ($2\frac{1}{2}$-inch squares), coarsely crumbled
- $1\frac{1}{2}$ cups semisweet chocolate chips
- 3 cups miniature marshmallows

Yummy, yummy! Kids will be rubbing their tummies to show how much they love these delicious cookies. The easy recipe combines rich peanut butter chips with flavorful pieces of crushed potato chips.

peanut butter-potato chip cookies

In a large bowl, cream butter and sugars until fluffy. Add eggs and vanilla; beat until smooth. Add flour; stir until a soft dough forms. Stir in peanut butter chips and potato chips.

Drop tablespoonfuls of dough 1 inch apart onto a greased baking sheet. Bake at 350° for 10 to 12 minutes or until edges are lightly browned. Transfer cookies to a wire rack to cool.

YIELD: about 8 dozen cookies

$1\frac{1}{4}$ cups butter or margarine, softened

1 cup firmly packed brown sugar

$\frac{1}{2}$ cup granulated sugar

2 eggs

1 teaspoon vanilla extract

$2\frac{3}{4}$ cups all-purpose flour

1 package (10 ounces) peanut butter chips

1 bag (7 ounces) rippled potato chips, coarsely crushed

These colorful cookies-on-a-stick are swirls of fun. Present them as surprise treats at children's parties, or prepare a batch of the moist cream cheese dough, divided and tinted in four bold colors, and let the kids have a party making their own!

fun lollipop cookies

In a large bowl, cream butter, cream cheese, and sugar until fluffy. Add egg and vanilla; beat until smooth. In a medium bowl, combine flour, baking powder, and salt. Add dry ingredients to creamed mixture; stir until a soft dough forms. Divide dough into fourths; tint pink, blue, green, and orange. Divide each color in half; wrap in plastic wrap and chill 2 hours.

Working with $1/2$ of each color of dough at a time, shape dough into $3/4$-inch balls. For each cookie, place 1 pink, blue, green, and orange balls side by side, pressing together gently. Shape into a 12-inch-long rope. Starting at one end, coil rope to make about a $2^3/4$-inch-diameter cookie. Place cookies 3 inches apart on a lightly greased baking sheet. Carefully insert lollipop sticks into bottoms of cookies. Bake at 350° for 8 to 10 minutes or until bottoms are lightly browned. Transfer cookies to a wire rack to cool.

YIELD: about $2^1/2$ dozen cookies

$3/4$ cup butter or margarine, softened

1 package (3 ounces) cream cheese, softened

1 cup sugar

1 egg

1 teaspoon vanilla extract

$2^3/4$ cups all-purpose flour

1 teaspoon baking powder

$1/4$ teaspoon salt

Pink, blue, green, and orange paste food colorings

Lollipop sticks

These tasty treats will score a home run with baseball fans!
The all-American peanut butter cookies are iced and decorated
with the red stitching of traditional baseballs.

baseball cookies

For cookies, cream butter, shortening, oil, and sugar until fluffy in a large bowl. Add eggs and vanilla; beat until smooth. Stir in peanut butter. In another large bowl, stir together flour and salt. Add dry ingredients to creamed mixture; stir until a soft dough forms. On a lightly floured surface, roll out dough to $1/4$-inch thickness. Use a 3-inch round cookie cutter to cut out cookies. Place on a greased baking sheet. Bake at 350° for 10 to 12 minutes or until bottoms are lightly browned. Transfer to a wire rack with waxed paper underneath to cool completely.

For icing, stir together sugar and milk until smooth in a small bowl; ice cookies. Allow icing to harden. Use a small round tip to pipe red icing on cookies to resemble stitching on a baseball. Allow icing to harden.

YIELD: about 5 dozen cookies

COOKIES

- 1 cup butter or margarine, softened
- $1/3$ cup butter-flavored shortening
- $1/3$ cup vegetable oil
- 2 cups granulated sugar
- 2 eggs
- 1 teaspoon vanilla extract
- 1 cup smooth peanut butter
- 5 cups all-purpose flour
- $1/2$ teaspoon salt

ICING

- 5 cups confectioners sugar
- 8 tablespoons milk
- 1 tube (4.25 ounces) red decorating icing and tip to fit tube

Featuring chewy oats and brown sugar, Chocolate-Peanut Butter Granola Squares hit the spot when youngsters need an energy boost. Bran muffin mix gives you a head-start on making them, and chocolate chips make them irresistible.

chocolate-peanut butter granola squares

In a medium bowl, combine muffin mix, oats, and brown sugar. With a pastry blender or 2 knives, cut in butter and peanut butter until mixture is well blended and crumbly. Stir in chocolate chips.

Press mixture into bottom of a 7 x 11-inch greased baking pan. Bake at 325° for 28 to 32 minutes or until golden brown and firm. Cool in pan on a wire rack.

Cut into 1½-inch squares.

YIELD: 2 dozen squares

1 package (7 ounces) bran muffin mix
½ cup old-fashioned oats
¼ cup firmly packed brown sugar
½ cup butter or margarine, softened
¼ cup crunchy peanut butter
½ cup semisweet chocolate chips

These maple-flavored United States maps are a neat – and yummy – teaching tool! Give hungry students a quick lesson in geography by having them guess which state is represented by the star-shaped candy sprinkle.

United States maps

In a large bowl, cream butter and sugars until fluffy. Add egg and maple flavoring; beat until smooth. In a small bowl, combine flour and salt. Add dry ingredients to creamed mixture; stir until a soft dough forms. Divide dough in half. Wrap in plastic wrap and chill 1 hour.

On a lightly floured surface, roll out $1/2$ of dough at a time to $1/4$-inch thickness. Use a 3 x 2-inch United States-shaped cookie cutter or pattern, page 140, and a sharp knife to cut out cookies. Place on a greased baking sheet. Place star-shaped sprinkles on cookies to represent different states. Bake at 350° for 6 to 8 minutes or until bottoms are lightly browned. Transfer cookies to a wire rack to cool.

YIELD: about 3 dozen cookies

$3/4$ cup butter or margarine, softened

$1/2$ cup confectioners sugar

$1/2$ cup firmly packed brown sugar

1 egg

1 teaspoon maple flavoring

$2 1/2$ cups all-purpose flour

$1/4$ teaspoon salt

Star-shaped sprinkles

Glow, little glowworm, glimmer, glimmer! Colored sugar crystals make these simple cookies shimmer and shine. Kids will love helping to shape them from refrigerated sugar cookie dough.

glowworms

Cut licorice into $\frac{1}{2}$-inch-long pieces; set aside.

Working with $\frac{1}{4}$ of dough at a time and keeping remainder in refrigerator, cut each portion into 12 pieces. Roll in sugar crystals and shape into 4-inch-long pencil-size ropes. Place ropes on a lightly greased baking sheet; shape to resemble worms. Bake at 350° for 6 to 8 minutes or until edges are lightly browned.

Press 2 pieces licorice into 1 end of each warm cookie for antennae. Transfer cookies to a wire rack to cool.

YIELD: about 4 dozen cookies

Red string licorice

1 package (16.5 ounces) refrigerated sugar cookie dough

Colored sugar crystals

HOLIDAYS

Colorful cookies go hand in hand with holiday celebrations!
Spread the fun with creative sweets that reflect the spirit of the day,
whether it be Valentine's Day, Easter, July 4th, or Halloween.

Resembling the popular Valentine's Day candies, these cute cookies let friends and loved ones do some fun flirting. Piped icing messages on the tinted cookies say it all with style and ease.

conversation heart cookies

For cookies, cream butter and confectioners sugar in a large bowl until fluffy. Add egg, vanilla, and butter flavoring; beat until smooth. In a medium bowl, combine flour and salt. Add dry ingredients to creamed mixture; stir until well blended. Divide dough into thirds; tint pink, light green, and yellow. Wrap in plastic wrap and chill 1 hour.

On a lightly floured surface, roll out $1/3$ of dough at a time to $1/4$-inch thickness. Use a 3-inch-wide heart-shaped cookie cutter to cut out cookies. Place on a greased baking sheet. Bake at 350° for 8 to 10 minutes or until bottoms are lightly browned. Transfer cookies to a wire rack to cool.

For icing, combine confectioners sugar, butter, shortening, milk, vanilla, and butter flavoring in a small bowl; beat until smooth. Stir in food coloring. Spoon icing into a decorating bag fitted with a small round tip. Pipe valentine messages onto cookies. Allow icing to harden.

YIELD: about 2 dozen cookies

COOKIES

- $3/4$ cup butter or margarine, softened
- 1 cup confectioners sugar
- 1 egg
- 1 teaspoon vanilla extract
- 1 teaspoon butter flavoring
- $2^1/2$ cups all-purpose flour
- $1/4$ teaspoon salt
- Red, green, and yellow liquid food colorings

ICING

- 1 cup confectioners sugar
- 1 tablespoon butter or margarine, softened
- $1/2$ tablespoon vegetable shortening
- 2 teaspoons milk
- $1/4$ teaspoon vanilla extract
- $1/4$ teaspoon butter flavoring
- $1^1/4$ teaspoons red liquid food coloring

O my love is like a red, red...cookie! Sizzling with red hot flavor, these boldly iced treats are blushing with tiny bits of chopped red cinnamon candies.

red hot valentines

Line a baking sheet with parchment paper; set aside.

For cookies, combine candies and sugar in a food processor; pulse process several times until candies are finely chopped. Add remaining ingredients to food processor; process 1 minute or until mixture is well blended. Shape dough into two 8-inch-long rolls. Wrap in plastic wrap and chill 2 hours or until firm.

Cut dough into 1/4-inch-thick slices. Place 2 inches apart on prepared baking sheet. Bake at 375° for 6 to 8 minutes or until edges are lightly browned. Cool cookies on baking sheet 2 minutes; transfer to a wire rack with waxed paper underneath to cool completely.

For icing, combine confectioners sugar and milk; beat until smooth. Tint red. Ice cookies. Allow icing to harden.

YIELD: about 4 dozen cookies

COOKIES

- 1/2 cup small red cinnamon candies
- 1/2 cup sugar
- 1 1/2 cups all-purpose flour
- 1/2 cup butter or margarine, softened
- 1 egg
- 1 teaspoon baking powder
- 1/8 teaspoon cinnamon-flavored oil (used in candy making)

ICING

- 3 1/2 cups confectioners sugar
- 5 tablespoons plus 1 teaspoon milk
- Red paste food coloring

With a bit of green for good luck on St. Patrick's Day, these rich chocolate cookies have a minty center that's fresh and cool. The centers and the sprinkles on top both are created using after-dinner layered chocolate mint candies.

chocolate-mint surprises

Line a baking sheet with parchment paper; set aside.

In a large bowl, cream butter and sugar until fluffy. Add sour cream, egg, and vanilla; beat until smooth. Stir in melted chocolate. In a small bowl, combine flour, baking powder, baking soda, and salt. Add dry ingredients to creamed mixture; stir until a soft dough forms.

Drop a scant $1/2$ tablespoonful of dough onto prepared baking sheet, place half a mint (cut mint into 2 squares) on dough, and top with another scant $1/2$ tablespoonful of dough. Repeat with remaining dough, placing cookies 3 inches apart. Bake at 350° for 9 to 11 minutes or until edges are crisp but centers are soft. Cool cookies on baking sheet 2 minutes; transfer to a wire rack to cool 10 minutes. While waiting, cut mints into small pieces; sprinkle on top of cookies. Cool completely.

YIELD: about $4^{1}/_{2}$ dozen cookies

$^{2}/_{3}$ cup butter or margarine, softened

$1^{2}/_{3}$ cups sugar

$1/_{2}$ cup sour cream

1 egg

1 teaspoon vanilla extract

2 ounces unsweetened baking chocolate, melted

$1^{3}/_{4}$ cups all-purpose flour

$1/_{2}$ teaspoon baking powder

$1/_{2}$ teaspoon baking soda

$1/_{4}$ teaspoon salt

Individually wrapped layered chocolate mints (about two 4.67-ounce packages)

Still searching for the leprechaun's pot of gold? Discovering these tasty cookies may well be the next best thing! Coated with gold-colored icing and sparkling sugar crystals, they have a wonderful orange flavor that is richly rewarding.

gold nuggets

For cookies, cream butter and confectioners sugar in a medium bowl until fluffy. Add egg, orange peel, and orange extract; beat until smooth. Gradually add flour; stir until a soft dough forms. Divide dough in half; shape each half into a 12-inch-long roll. Wrap in plastic wrap and chill 1 hour.

Cut dough into 1/2-inch-thick slices. Place on a greased baking sheet. Bake at 325° for 12 to 15 minutes or until bottoms are lightly browned. Transfer cookies to a wire rack with waxed paper underneath to cool completely.

For icing, stir confectioners sugar and milk together in a small bowl until smooth. Tint icing gold. Using a fork, dip entire cookie into icing and return to wire rack. Sprinkle with sugar crystals before icing hardens. Allow icing to harden.

YIELD: about 4 dozen cookies

COOKIES

- 1/2 cup butter, softened
- 3/4 cup confectioners sugar
- 1 egg
- 1 teaspoon dried grated orange peel
- 1 teaspoon orange extract
- 1 3/4 cups all-purpose flour

ICING

- 2 1/2 cups confectioners sugar
- 5 tablespoons milk
- Gold paste food coloring
- Gold sugar crystals

Here comes Peter Cottontail, Hoppin' down the bunny trail, Hippity hoppin', Easter's on its way! Accented with jelly bean tails and ears, these lightly sweet cookies will help spread "hoppy" Easter wishes.

springtime bunnies

In a large bowl, cream butter and sugars until fluffy. Add egg and vanilla; beat until smooth. In a medium bowl, combine flour, baking soda, and cream of tartar. Add dry ingredients to creamed mixture; stir until a soft dough forms. Divide dough in half. Wrap in plastic wrap and chill 2 hours.

On a lightly floured surface, roll out $1/2$ of dough at a time to slightly less than $1/4$-inch thickness. Use a 4-inch-wide x $3^1/_4$-inch-high cookie cutter or pattern, page 140, and a sharp knife to cut out cookies. Place 2 inches apart on a lightly greased baking sheet. Press jelly beans into cookies for ears and tails. Bake at 350° for 8 to 10 minutes or until bottoms are lightly browned. Transfer cookies to a wire rack to cool.

YIELD: about 2 dozen cookies

- $3/4$ **cup butter or margarine, softened**
- $1/2$ **cup granulated sugar**
- $1/2$ **cup confectioners sugar**
- 1 **egg**
- $1^1/_2$ **teaspoons vanilla extract**
- $2^1/_4$ **cups all-purpose flour**
- $1/2$ **teaspoon baking soda**
- $1/2$ **teaspoon cream of tartar**
  Pink and white gourmet jelly beans

Here's a delicious alternative to decorating Easter eggs: bake a batch of egg-shaped cookies that you paint with paste food coloring! Squiggles, swirls, lines, and dots are an easy way to dress up the buttery cookies, but you can be as artsy as you please.

easter egg cookies

In a large bowl, cream butter and sugar until fluffy. Add egg and extracts; beat until smooth. In a small bowl, combine flour, baking powder, and salt. Add dry ingredients to creamed mixture; stir until a soft dough forms. Wrap in plastic wrap and chill 1 hour.

On a lightly floured surface, roll out dough to $1/8$-inch thickness. Use a $1^1/2$ x $2^1/2$-inch egg-shaped cookie cutter to cut out cookies. Place on a lightly greased baking sheet. Bake at 350° for 7 to 9 minutes or until bottoms are lightly browned. Transfer cookies to a wire rack to cool.

Place 1 teaspoon of water in each of 3 small bowls; tint dark pink, violet, and yellow. Paint desired designs on cookies using a small, clean paintbrush for each color; allow designs to dry.

YIELD: about $4^1/2$ dozen cookies

$1/2$ cup butter or margarine, softened
$1/2$ cup sugar
1 egg
$1/2$ teaspoon vanilla extract
$1/4$ teaspoon lemon extract
$1^2/3$ cups all-purpose flour
$1/2$ teaspoon baking powder
$1/4$ teaspoon salt
Pink, violet, and yellow paste food colorings

Hooray for the Red, White, and Blue! These fun cookies are simply layers of tinted dough that are stacked and cut into "ribbons" before baking. Finely ground toasted pecans enhance the taste.

patriotic ribbons

Line two 4 x 8-inch loaf pans with waxed paper, extending paper over sides; lightly grease paper. Set aside.

In a large bowl, cream butter and sugar until fluffy. Add egg and vanilla; beat until smooth. In a medium bowl, combine flour, baking powder, and salt. Add dry ingredients to creamed mixture; stir until a soft dough forms. Stir in pecans. Divide dough into thirds. Tint $1/3$ of dough red and $1/3$ of dough blue. Press $1/2$ of blue dough into bottom of each pan. Press plain dough over blue dough. Press red dough over plain dough. Cover pans with plastic wrap and chill overnight.

Use waxed paper to lift dough from each pan. Cut dough into $1/4$-inch-thick slices. Place 2 inches apart on an ungreased nonstick baking sheet. Bake at 375° for 8 to 10 minutes or until bottoms are lightly browned. Transfer cookies to a wire rack to cool.

YIELD: about 4 dozen cookies

1 cup butter or margarine, softened

$1^1/4$ cups sugar

1 egg

1 teaspoon vanilla extract

$2^1/2$ cups all-purpose flour

$1^1/2$ teaspoons baking powder

$1/2$ teaspoon salt

1 cup chopped pecans, toasted and finely ground

$1/4$ teaspoon *each* red and blue paste food colorings

Hauntingly good treats, these cookies are also fun for decorating your Halloween party table. The glazed Ghost Cookies are finished with friendly piped-on faces. The Spiced Pumpkin Cookies are capped with creamy brown sugar icing.

ghost cookies

For cookies, cream butter and sugars until fluffy in a medium bowl. Add milk, egg, and vanilla; beat until smooth. In a small bowl, combine flour, baking powder, and salt. Add dry ingredients to creamed mixture; stir until well blended. Divide dough into thirds. Wrap in plastic wrap and chill 2 hours.

On a lightly floured surface, roll out $1/3$ of dough at a time to slightly less than $1/4$-inch thickness. Use pattern, page 141, and a sharp knife to cut out cookies. Place 1 inch apart on a lightly greased baking sheet. Bake at 400° for 5 to 7 minutes or until bottoms are lightly browned. Transfer cookies to a wire rack with waxed paper underneath to cool.

For white icing, combine confectioners sugar, water, corn syrup, and vanilla in a large bowl; stir until smooth. Spoon icing over cookies; allow icing to harden.

Use black icing tube fitted with a small round tip to pipe eyes, nose, and mouth onto each cookie. Use orange icing tube fitted with a small round tip to pipe a bow onto each cookie. Store in a single layer.

YIELD: about 14 cookies

COOKIES

- $1/2$ cup butter or margarine, softened
- $3/4$ cup granulated sugar
- $1/4$ cup firmly packed brown sugar
- $1/4$ cup milk
- 1 egg
- $1 1/2$ teaspoons vanilla extract
- 2 cups all-purpose flour
- $1/2$ teaspoon baking powder
- $1/2$ teaspoon salt

ICING

- 5 cups confectioners sugar
- 6 to 7 tablespoons water
- 1 tablespoon light corn syrup
- 1 teaspoon vanilla extract
- 1 tube (4.25 ounces) black decorating icing
- 1 tube (4.25 ounces) orange decorating icing
- Decorating tips to fit icing tubes

spiced pumpkin cookies

COOKIES

- $1/2$ cup butter or margarine, softened
- $1 1/2$ cups firmly packed brown sugar
- $3/4$ cup canned pumpkin
- 1 egg
- 1 tablespoon grated orange zest
- $1 1/4$ cups all-purpose flour
- $1 1/4$ cups whole-wheat flour
- 1 teaspoon pumpkin pie spice
- 1 teaspoon baking soda
- $1/4$ teaspoon salt
- 2 cups chopped walnuts

ICING

- $1/2$ cup butter or margarine
- 1 cup firmly packed brown sugar
- $1/4$ cup whipping cream
- 1 tablespoon light corn syrup
- 1 cup confectioners sugar

continued on next page

Baked on lollipop sticks, orange-flavored Pumpkin Cookie Pops will have little goblins grinning!
They get their expressive faces from chocolate batter that is piped on before baking.

pumpkin cookie pops

In a large bowl, cream $1/2$ cup butter, cream cheese, and sugar until fluffy. Add egg and extracts; beat until smooth. Tint dough orange. In a medium bowl, combine $2^{1}/_{2}$ cups flour, baking powder, and salt. Add dry ingredients to creamed mixture; stir until a soft dough forms. Divide dough in half. Wrap in plastic wrap and chill 2 hours.

On a lightly floured surface, roll out $1/2$ of dough at a time to $3/8$-inch thickness. Use a $2^{1}/_{4}$-inch-diameter pumpkin-shaped cookie cutter or pattern, page 140, and a sharp knife to cut out cookies. Place on a lightly greased baking sheet. Carefully insert a lollipop stick into the bottom of each cookie.

In a small bowl, combine remaining $1/4$ cup butter, remaining $1/4$ cup flour, and chocolate syrup; stir until well blended. Spoon chocolate mixture into a decorating bag fitted with a small round tip. Pipe a pumpkin face onto each cookie. Bake at 350° for 8 to 10 minutes or until bottoms are lightly browned. Transfer cookies to a wire rack to cool.

YIELD: about $2^{1}/_{2}$ dozen cookies

$3/4$ cup butter or margarine, softened and divided

1 package (3 ounces) cream cheese, softened

1 cup sugar

1 egg

1 teaspoon orange extract

$1/2$ teaspoon vanilla extract

Orange paste food coloring

$2^{3}/_{4}$ cups all-purpose flour, divided

1 teaspoon baking powder

$1/4$ teaspoon salt

$4^{1}/_{2}$-inch lollipop sticks

1 tablespoon chocolate syrup

spiced pumpkin cookies (continued)

For cookies, cream butter and brown sugar in a large bowl until fluffy. Add pumpkin, egg, and orange zest; beat until smooth. In a medium bowl, combine flours, pumpkin pie spice, baking soda, and salt. Add dry ingredients to creamed mixture; stir until a soft dough forms. Stir in walnuts. Wrap in plastic wrap and chill 4 hours.

Drop tablespoonfuls of dough 2 inches apart onto a greased baking sheet. Bake at 375° for 10 to 12 minutes or until bottoms are lightly browned. Transfer cookies to a wire rack to cool.

For icing, melt butter in a heavy medium saucepan over medium heat. Stirring constantly, add brown sugar, whipping cream, and corn syrup; cook until mixture comes to a boil. Boil 1 minute. Remove from heat; pour into a heat-resistant medium bowl. Add confectioners sugar and beat until smooth. Ice cookies; allow icing to harden.

YIELD: about 5 dozen cookies

Make your harvest celebrations sweet with Maple-Nut Wreaths, pretty cookies that look like tiny pecan pies. A rich and creamy butterscotch topping enhances Walnut Spice Bars, which have a moist, spicy crust.

maple-nut wreaths

Line a baking sheet with parchment paper; set aside.

In a large bowl, cream butter and sugar until fluffy. Add egg and vanilla; beat until smooth. Add flour; stir until a soft dough forms. Place $1/2$ cup of dough in a small bowl. Stir in pecans and maple syrup, mixing well; set aside.

Working in batches, place remaining dough in a cookie press fitted with a star plate. Press dough into 4-inch lengths onto prepared baking sheet. Join ends of each dough length to form a wreath. Place about 1 teaspoon pecan mixture into center of each wreath. Bake at 350° for 10 to 15 minutes or until bottoms are lightly browned. Transfer cookies to a wire rack to cool.

YIELD: about 5 dozen cookies

1 cup butter or margarine, softened
$1/2$ cup sugar
1 egg
1 teaspoon vanilla extract
$2 1/2$ cups all-purpose flour
2 cups chopped pecans, toasted and finely ground
$1/2$ cup maple syrup

walnut spice bars

Line a 9 x 13-inch baking pan with waxed paper; lightly grease paper. Set aside.

For crust, combine cake mix, oil, applesauce, egg, and vanilla in a medium bowl. Spread mixture into prepared pan. Bake at 350° for 20 to 25 minutes or until edges are lightly browned. While crust is baking, prepare topping.

For topping, combine sugar, butter, and milk in a heavy medium saucepan over medium-high heat. Stirring constantly, bring mixture to a boil and boil 1 minute. Remove from heat and add butterscotch chips; stir until smooth. Stir in walnuts. Spread hot topping over warm crust. Cool in pan. Cut into 1 x 2-inch bars.

YIELD: about 4 dozen bars

CRUST
1 package (18.25 ounces) spice cake mix
$1/3$ cup vegetable oil
$1/3$ cup applesauce
1 egg
1 teaspoon vanilla extract

TOPPING
1 cup sugar
$1/3$ cup butter or margarine
$1/3$ cup milk
1 cup butterscotch chips
1 cup chopped walnuts

CHRISTMAS

For sharing holiday joy, you can't beat cookies!
Their sweet flavors and exciting textures always bring on smiles
and call up warm, delicious memories of Christmases past.

Ho, ho, ho! These Santa Cookies are ready to party! Sure to delight young and old alike,
the star-shaped cutouts are decorated with colorful icing and bits of licorice.

santa cookies

For cookies, cream butter, shortening, sugar, and vanilla in a large mixing bowl. Beat in eggs, one at a time, beating well after each addition. Stir in flour and cream of tartar. Wrap in plastic wrap and chill at least 2 hours.

On a lightly floured surface, roll out dough to $1/8$-inch thickness. Use a 3-inch-wide star-shaped cookie cutter or pattern, page 141, and a sharp knife to cut out cookies. Place on a lightly greased baking sheet. Bake at 425° for 6 to 8 minutes or until edges are lightly browned. Transfer cookies to a wire rack to cool.

For icing, combine all ingredients except food coloring in a medium mixing bowl, blending until smooth. Divide icing in half; tint $1/2$ red. Referring to photo, ice cookies with red icing. Spoon white icing into a decorating bag fitted with a small round tip and pipe beards and trims. Use icing to attach small pieces of licorice for eyes.

YIELD: about 6 dozen cookies

COOKIES

- $1/2$ cup butter or margarine, softened
- $1/2$ cup vegetable shortening
- 1 cup granulated sugar
- $1 1/2$ teaspoons vanilla extract
- 3 eggs
- $3 1/2$ cups all-purpose flour
- 2 teaspoons cream of tartar

ICING

- 3 cups confectioners sugar
- $1/4$ cup butter or margarine, softened
- $1/4$ cup milk
- 1 teaspoon vanilla extract
- Red paste food coloring
- Small pieces of black licorice for eyes

The symbolic shape and tempting scent of cinnamon make our Spicy Christmas Tree Cookies a treat the whole family can enjoy. For a cozy presentation, arrange a plateful of cookies to resemble a patchwork quilt block.

spicy Christmas tree cookies

Combine brown sugar and molasses in a heavy small saucepan. Stirring constantly, cook over medium-high heat until mixture boils. Boil 1 minute; remove from heat. In a large bowl, combine butter and hot sugar mixture; stir until butter melts. Add egg and orange extract; beat until well blended. In a medium bowl, combine flour, cinnamon, cardamom, and baking soda. Add dry ingredients to butter mixture; stir until well blended. Divide dough into thirds. Wrap in plastic wrap and chill 2 hours.

On a lightly floured surface, roll out $1/3$ of dough at a time into a 9 x 14-inch piece. Make 3-inch-wide lengthwise cuts with a knife. Use a scalloped-edge pastry cutter to make a diagonal cut from upper left corner to $4^1/8$ inches from lower left corner (*Fig. 1*). Make a second diagonal cut $2^3/4$ inches from first cut (*Fig. 2*). Continue making diagonal cuts $2^3/4$ inches from previous cuts. Refer to **Fig. 3** to make diagonal cuts $2^3/4$ inches apart, beginning at upper left corner to form triangles. Place on a lightly greased baking sheet. Bake at 350° for 5 to 7 minutes or until edges are lightly browned. Transfer cookies to a wire rack to cool.

Use red icing tube fitted with a small round tip to pipe designs onto cookies. Allow icing to harden.

YIELD: about $6^1/2$ dozen cookies

$2/3$ cup firmly packed brown sugar

$1/3$ cup molasses

$3/4$ cup butter or margarine

1 egg

1 teaspoon orange extract

$3^1/2$ cups all-purpose flour

2 teaspoons ground cinnamon

$1/2$ teaspoon ground cardamom

$1/2$ teaspoon baking soda

1 tube (4.25 ounces) red decorating icing and tip to fit tube

Fig. 1

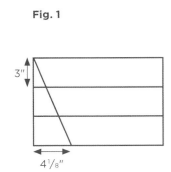

3"

$4^1/8$"

Fig. 2

$2^3/4$"

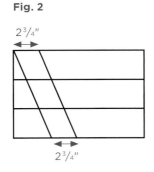

$2^3/4$"

Fig. 3

$2^3/4$"

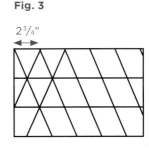

Iced in bright colors, these Round Ornament Cookies are great for multitasking: serve them to guests, wrap up a boxful for gift-giving, or add ribbon loops for hanging on a small tree. You probably already have the ingredients you need to make them.

round ornament cookies

For cookies, cream butter, shortening, and sugars in a large bowl until fluffy. Add corn syrup, egg, and vanilla; beat until smooth. In a medium bowl, combine flour and salt. Add dry ingredients to creamed mixture; stir until a soft dough forms. Divide dough in half. On a lightly floured surface, roll out $1/2$ of dough at a time to $1/8$-inch thickness. Use pattern, page 142, and a sharp knife to cut out cookies. Place on a greased baking sheet. Use a plastic drinking straw to cut a hole in the top of each cookie. Bake at 350° for 6 to 8 minutes or until bottoms are lightly browned. Transfer cookies to a wire rack to cool.

For icing, combine confectioners sugar, water, corn syrup, and vanilla in a medium bowl; stir until smooth. Place $1/4$ cup white icing in a small bowl and cover. Divide remaining icing into 4 small bowls; tint icing red, green, yellow, and blue. Spoon icing into decorating bags fitted with small round tips. Use tinted icing to pipe outline around edges of cookies; fill in with icing. Allow icing to harden. Use white icing to pipe a "highlight" on each cookie. Store in a single layer.

YIELD: about $4 1/2$ dozen cookies

COOKIES

- $1/2$ cup butter or margarine, softened
- $1/3$ cup vegetable shortening
- $1/2$ cup granulated sugar
- $1/2$ cup firmly packed brown sugar
- $1/4$ cup dark corn syrup
- 1 egg
- 1 teaspoon vanilla extract
- 3 cups all-purpose flour
- $1/4$ teaspoon salt

ICING

- $6 2/3$ cups confectioners sugar
- $1/2$ cup water
- 1 tablespoon light corn syrup
- 1 teaspoon vanilla extract
  Red, green, yellow, and blue paste food colorings

These cookies are real treasures! Bite-Size Snowball Macaroons will melt in your mouth. Christmas Jewels are buttery piped cookies accented with colorful jelly beans.

bite-size snowball macaroons

In a medium bowl, combine $\frac{1}{4}$ cup sugar, flour, and salt. Stir in coconut. In another medium bowl, beat egg whites until soft peaks form; add vanilla. Gradually add remaining 1 cup sugar; continue to beat until mixture is very stiff. Gently fold coconut mixture into egg white mixture.

Drop $\frac{1}{2}$ teaspoonfuls of mixture onto a lightly greased baking sheet. Bake at 325° for 9 to 11 minutes or until bottoms are lightly browned. Transfer cookies to a wire rack to cool.

YIELD: about 10 dozen macaroons

$1\frac{1}{4}$ cups sugar, divided
$\frac{1}{2}$ cup all-purpose flour
$\frac{1}{4}$ teaspoon salt
$2\frac{1}{2}$ cups sweetened flaked coconut
4 egg whites
$\frac{1}{2}$ teaspoon vanilla extract

Christmas jewels

Line a greased baking sheet with parchment paper; set aside.

In a large bowl, cream butter and sugar until fluffy. Add egg and vanilla; beat until smooth. In a medium bowl, combine flour and baking powder. Add dry ingredients to creamed mixture; stir until a soft dough forms.

Spoon dough into a decorating bag fitted with a large open star tip (#6B). Pipe 2-inch-long shells onto prepared baking sheet. Press a jelly bean into small end of each shell. Bake at 400° for 6 to 8 minutes or until bottoms are lightly browned. Transfer cookies to a wire rack to cool.

YIELD: about 6 dozen cookies

$1\frac{1}{2}$ cups butter or margarine, softened
1 cup sugar
1 egg
2 teaspoons vanilla extract
3 cups all-purpose flour
1 teaspoon baking powder
Red and green jelly beans

Run, run, as fast as you can…or these gingerbread boys and girls all will be gone. It's hard to resist their sweet personalities and spicy aroma! For extra fun, make cookie ornaments that children can use to create edible necklace party favors.

gingerbread cookies

For cookies, cream butter, shortening, and brown sugar in a large bowl until fluffy. Add buttermilk, molasses, eggs, and vanilla; beat until well blended. In another large bowl, combine remaining ingredients. Add half of dry ingredients to creamed mixture; stir until a soft dough forms. Stir in remaining dry ingredients, 1 cup at a time; use hands if necessary to mix well. Divide dough into fourths. Wrap in plastic wrap and chill 2 hours or until dough is firm.

On a lightly floured surface, roll out $1/4$ of dough at a time to slightly less than $1/4$-inch thickness. Use a cookie cutter (7-inch-high gingerbread man and/or a $2^1/2$-inch-wide heart) to cut out cookies. Place on a greased baking sheet. If making necklaces, use a plastic drinking straw to cut a hole in the top of each heart. Bake at 350° for 7 to 9 minutes or until firm. Transfer cookies to a wire rack to cool.

For icing, combine all ingredients in a small bowl; stir until smooth. Spoon icing into a decorating bag fitted with a small round tip. Decorate cookies with icing and desired candies. Allow icing to harden.

For heart necklaces, use a plastic yarn needle with a large eye to string gumdrops and small, round candies (with holes in the centers) onto narrow ribbon. Use ribbon to tie wrapped peppermints and a cookie heart to each necklace.

YIELD: about $1^1/2$ dozen 7-inch cookies or about $6^1/2$ dozen $2^1/2$-inch heart cookies

COOKIES

- $2/3$ cup butter or margarine, softened
- $1/3$ cup vegetable shortening
- $3/4$ cup firmly packed brown sugar
- $1/2$ cup buttermilk
- $1/2$ cup molasses
- 2 eggs
- 1 teaspoon vanilla extract
- $5^1/4$ cups all-purpose flour
- $1/4$ cup cocoa
- 2 teaspoons ground cinnamon
- $1^1/2$ teaspoons ground ginger
- 1 teaspoon ground allspice
- 1 teaspoon baking powder
- 1 teaspoon baking soda
- 1 teaspoon salt

ICING

- $1^1/2$ cups confectioners sugar
- 5 teaspoons water
- Candies to decorate
- Narrow ribbon for heart necklaces

Diamond-shaped shortbread "Stained Glass" Cookies are doubly dazzling with the rich taste of their glazed topping of candied fruit and chopped pecans. Delicious Christmas Mincemeat Bars have a crumbly crust and topping made with oats and cake mix.

"stained glass" cookies

Line a 10^1/$_2$ x 15^1/$_2$-inch jellyroll pan with heavy aluminum foil, extending foil over sides of pan; lightly grease foil. Set aside.

In a large bowl, cream butter and sugar until fluffy. Add egg and vanilla; beat until smooth. In a medium bowl, combine flour and salt. Add dry ingredients to creamed mixture; stir until a soft dough forms. Press dough into bottom of prepared pan. In a medium bowl, combine candied fruit and pecans. Sprinkle fruit mixture over dough; lightly press into dough. Bake at 375° for 22 to 24 minutes or until edges are lightly browned. Use ends of foil to lift from pan; allow to cool.

In a small saucepan, bring corn syrup to a boil. Boil 1 minute. Brush corn syrup over top of cookies; cool completely. Follow Cutting Diamond-Shaped Bars, page 139, to cut bars.

YIELD: about 4 dozen bars

- 1 cup butter or margarine, softened
- 1^1/$_2$ cups sugar
- 1 egg
- 1 teaspoon vanilla extract
- 2^3/$_4$ cups all-purpose flour
- ^{1}/$_4$ teaspoon salt
- 1 pound chopped mixed candied fruit
- 2 cups chopped pecans
- ^{1}/$_4$ cup light corn syrup

Christmas mincemeat bars

In a medium bowl, combine cake mix, oats, and melted butter (mixture will be crumbly). Reserving 2 cups oat mixture, firmly press remaining mixture into bottom of a lightly greased 9 x 13-inch baking pan. Spread mincemeat over crust. Sprinkle reserved oat mixture over mincemeat. Bake at 375° for 30 to 35 minutes or until topping is lightly browned. Cool in pan on a wire rack. Cut into 1 x 2-inch bars.

YIELD: about 4 dozen bars

- 1 package (18.25 ounces) yellow cake mix
- 2^1/$_2$ cups quick-cooking oats
- ^{3}/$_4$ cup butter or margarine, melted
- 1 jar (27 ounces) mincemeat

If you've been to Germany's famous Christkindl Market, you'll recognize these festive star cookies. The Bavarian favorites are decorated with candied cherries and either blanched whole almonds or walnut halves.

spiced Christmas stars

In a large bowl, cream butter and brown sugar until fluffy. Add eggs and honey; beat until smooth. In a medium bowl, combine flour, cornstarch, cinnamon, baking soda, ginger, nutmeg, and salt. Gradually add dry ingredients to creamed mixture; stir until a soft dough forms. Divide dough in half. Wrap in plastic wrap and chill 2 hours.

On a lightly floured surface, roll out $1/2$ of dough at a time to $1/4$-inch thickness. Use a 4-inch-wide star-shaped cookie cutter or pattern, page 142, and a sharp knife to cut out cookies. Place 2 inches apart on a greased baking sheet. Cut a $3/4$-inch-diameter hole in center of each cookie. Decorate tops of cookies with cherries and almonds or walnuts. Bake at 350° for 6 to 8 minutes or until golden brown. Transfer cookies to a wire rack to cool.

YIELD: about 2 dozen cookies

- $1/2$ cup butter or margarine, softened
- $1/2$ cup firmly packed brown sugar
- 2 eggs
- $1/2$ cup honey
- $3 1/2$ cups all-purpose flour
- $1/4$ cup cornstarch
- $1 1/2$ teaspoons ground cinnamon
- 1 teaspoon baking soda
- $1/2$ teaspoon ground ginger
- $1/4$ teaspoon ground nutmeg
- $1/4$ teaspoon salt
- Red and green candied cherries, halved
- Blanched whole almonds
- Walnut halves

Spiked Eggnog Brownies are a tempting treat for holiday merry-makers. The extra-moist cakes feature eggnog and bourbon both in the brownies and in their creamy topping.

spiked eggnog brownies

Line a greased 10$\frac{1}{2}$ x 15$\frac{1}{2}$-inch jellyroll pan with waxed paper; set aside.

For brownies, combine butter, water, and oil in a heavy small saucepan over medium-high heat. Bring to a boil. Remove from heat. In a medium bowl, combine flour, sugar, cocoa, baking powder, and salt. Add butter mixture to dry ingredients; stir until well blended. In a small bowl, whisk together eggnog, bourbon, and eggs; stir into batter. Pour into prepared pan. Bake at 400° for 12 to 14 minutes or until a toothpick inserted near center comes out clean. Cool in pan. Cut into 2-inch squares.

For icing, combine all ingredients in a medium bowl. Beat until well blended and smooth. Spoon icing into a decorating bag fitted with a large open star tip (#19). Pipe a large dollop of icing onto center of each brownie. Cover and store in refrigerator.

YIELD: about 3 dozen brownies

BROWNIES

- $\frac{1}{2}$ cup butter or margarine
- $\frac{1}{2}$ cup water
- $\frac{1}{2}$ cup vegetable oil
- 2 cups all-purpose flour
- 2 cups sugar
- $\frac{1}{4}$ cup cocoa
- $\frac{1}{2}$ teaspoon baking powder
- $\frac{1}{8}$ teaspoon salt
- $\frac{1}{2}$ cup eggnog
- $\frac{1}{2}$ cup bourbon
- 2 eggs

ICING

- 2 cups confectioners sugar
- 6 tablespoons butter or margarine, softened
- $\frac{1}{4}$ cup vegetable shortening
- 2 tablespoons eggnog
- 2 teaspoons bourbon
- $\frac{1}{8}$ teaspoon freshly grated nutmeg

Candied fruits and chopped walnuts bring traditional Christmas flavor to Chewy Fruitcake Bars and soft Pineapple Jumbles. Shredded coconut enhances the moist sweets.

pineapple jumbles

In a large bowl, cream butter and sugars until fluffy. Add sour cream, egg, and vanilla; beat until smooth. In a small bowl, combine flour, baking soda, and salt. Add dry ingredients to creamed mixture; stir until a soft dough forms. Stir in remaining ingredients.

Drop tablespoonfuls of dough 2 inches apart onto a greased baking sheet. Bake at 350° for 10 to 12 minutes or until edges are lightly browned. Transfer cookies to a wire rack to cool.

YIELD: about 4 dozen cookies

- ½ cup butter or margarine, softened
- ½ cup granulated sugar
- ½ cup firmly packed brown sugar
- ½ cup sour cream
- 1 egg
- 1 teaspoon vanilla extract
- 1¼ cups all-purpose flour
- ¼ teaspoon baking soda
- ¼ teaspoon salt
- 1 cup sweetened shredded coconut
- 1 cup coarsely chopped walnuts
- 1 cup finely chopped candied pineapple

chewy fruitcake bars

In a large bowl, cream butter and brown sugar until fluffy. Add flour; stir until a soft dough forms. Press dough into the bottom of a greased 9 x 13-inch baking pan. Bake at 350° for 10 minutes.

Place walnuts, dates, coconut, cherries, and pineapple in food processor. Pulse process until mixture is coarsely chopped. Reserving 1 cup fruit mixture, spoon remaining mixture over crust. Pour sweetened condensed milk over fruit mixture. Sprinkle reserved mixture on top. Bake at 350° for 30 more minutes or until top is lightly browned. Cool in pan 15 minutes.

Cut into 1 x 2-inch bars while warm; cool completely in pan.

YIELD: about 4 dozen bars

- ½ cup butter or margarine, softened
- ⅓ cup firmly packed brown sugar
- 1 cup all-purpose flour
- 1 cup chopped walnuts
- 1 cup chopped dates
- 1 cup sweetened shredded coconut
- ½ cup green candied cherries
- ½ cup red candied cherries
- ½ cup candied pineapple
- 1 can (14 ounces) sweetened condensed milk

With their hearty flavor and crunchy texture, these delicious goodies will be loved by all. Crushed cinnamon graham crackers and dry-roasted peanuts are the surprise ingredients.

peanut butter crumb cookies

In a large bowl, cream butter, peanut butter, and sugars until fluffy. Add eggs and vanilla; beat until smooth. In a medium bowl, combine flour, baking powder, baking soda, and salt. Add dry ingredients to creamed mixture; beat until well blended. Stir in 1 cup cracker crumbs.

In a small bowl, combine remaining $1/2$ cup cracker crumbs and peanuts. Shape dough into 1-inch balls; roll in crumb mixture. Place balls 2 inches apart on a lightly greased baking sheet; flatten balls in a crisscross pattern with a fork. Bake at 350° for 7 to 9 minutes or until bottoms are lightly browned. Transfer cookies to a wire rack to cool.

YIELD: about 7 dozen cookies

- 1 cup butter or margarine, softened
- 1 cup crunchy peanut butter
- $3/4$ cup firmly packed brown sugar
- $3/4$ cup granulated sugar
- 2 eggs
- $1 1/2$ teaspoons vanilla extract
- $2 1/2$ cups all-purpose flour
- 1 teaspoon baking powder
- 1 teaspoon baking soda
- $1/2$ teaspoon salt
- $1 1/2$ cups coarsely crushed cinnamon graham crackers (about 22 squares), divided
- $1/2$ cup finely chopped dry-roasted peanuts

ELEGANT CLASSICS

Any cookie is hard to resist, but those with sophisticated flavors and textures are extra enticing. These choices feature sensational tastes that will keep people coming back for more!

Some things are just meant to be together, and the flavors of orange and chocolate are high on the list of favorite combinations. Glistening with sugar, these thin and crispy orange cookies are dipped in melted chocolate for a dramatic finish.

chocolate-dipped orange melts

In a large bowl, cream butter and 1 cup sugar until fluffy. Add egg, 1/2 teaspoon orange extract, and vanilla; beat until smooth. In a medium bowl, combine flour, baking powder, and salt. Add dry ingredients to creamed mixture; stir until a soft dough forms.

Shape dough into 1-inch balls and place 2 inches apart on an ungreased baking sheet. Flatten balls with bottom of a glass that has been greased and dipped in sugar. Bake at 375° for 5 to 7 minutes or until edges are lightly browned. Transfer cookies to a wire rack to cool.

Line a baking sheet with waxed paper; set aside. In a small saucepan, melt chocolate chips and shortening over low heat, stirring constantly. Remove from heat and stir in remaining 1/2 teaspoon orange extract. Dip 1/2 of each cookie into melted chocolate. Place on prepared baking sheet and chill until chocolate hardens. Store in single layers between sheets of waxed paper and in a cool place.

YIELD: about 6 dozen cookies

- 1 cup butter or margarine, softened
- 1 cup sugar
- 1 egg
- 1 teaspoon orange extract, divided
- 1/2 teaspoon vanilla extract
- 2 1/4 cups all-purpose flour
- 1 teaspoon baking powder
- 1/4 teaspoon salt
- Sugar
- 1 package (12 ounces) semisweet chocolate chips
- 1 tablespoon vegetable shortening

Definitely delicious, Almond Delights are rich cookies of creamy almond-flavored dough topped with chocolate-covered whole almonds. The melt-in-your-mouth Hazelnut Macaroons follow tradition with their crisp, crunchy outer and soft center.

hazelnut macaroons

Line a baking sheet with parchment paper; set aside.

In a medium bowl, beat egg whites until soft peaks form. Add vanilla and cream of tartar. Gradually add sugar, beating until mixture is very stiff. Gently fold hazelnuts into egg white mixture.

Drop teaspoonfuls of mixture 2 inches apart onto prepared baking sheet. Bake at 300° for 17 to 20 minutes or until bottoms are lightly browned. Transfer cookies to a wire rack to cool.

YIELD: about 5^1/$_2$ dozen cookies

- 3 egg whites
- ^{1}/$_2$ teaspoon vanilla extract
- ^{1}/$_2$ teaspoon cream of tartar
- 1 cup sugar
- 1^2/$_3$ cups finely ground hazelnuts

almond delights

In a large bowl, cream butter, cream cheese, and sugar until fluffy. Add egg yolk and almond extract; beat until smooth. Add flour to creamed mixture; stir until a soft dough forms. Wrap in plastic wrap and chill 1 hour.

Shape dough into 1-inch balls and place 2 inches apart on a greased baking sheet. Use thumb or the back of a small, round measuring spoon to make a slight indentation in each ball. Bake at 350° for 12 to 15 minutes or until bottoms are lightly browned. Press 1 almond into center of each warm cookie. Transfer cookies to a wire rack to cool.

YIELD: about 6 dozen cookies

- 1 cup butter or margarine, softened
- 1 package (3 ounces) cream cheese, softened
- 1 cup sugar
- 1 egg yolk
- 1 teaspoon almond extract
- 2^1/$_2$ cups all-purpose flour
- 1 cup chocolate-covered whole almonds

When you sink your teeth into these moist, nutty bars, your taste buds will be in ecstasy! The buttery brown sugar crust is covered with a rich, dense mixture of toasted pecans enhanced with pecan liqueur.

pecan-praline bars

For crust, cream butter and brown sugar in a medium bowl until fluffy. Add flour; stir until well blended. Press crust into bottom of a lightly greased 9 x 13-inch baking pan. Bake at 350° for 12 minutes.

For topping, combine brown sugar and eggs in a medium bowl; beat until well blended. In a small bowl, combine flour and baking powder. Add dry ingredients, liqueur, and vanilla to brown sugar mixture; stir until well blended. Stir in pecans and pour over warm crust. Bake at 350° for 20 to 25 minutes or until center is set and top is golden brown. Place pan on a wire rack to cool. Cut into 1 x 2-inch bars.

YIELD: about 4 dozen bars

CRUST

- $3/4$ cup butter or margarine, softened
- $1/3$ cup firmly packed brown sugar
- $1^1/2$ cups all-purpose flour

TOPPING

- $1^1/2$ cups firmly packed brown sugar
- 3 eggs, beaten
- 3 tablespoons all-purpose flour
- $1/2$ teaspoon baking powder
- 3 tablespoons pecan liqueur
- 1 teaspoon vanilla extract
- $1^1/2$ cups coarsely chopped pecans, toasted

Light, delicate Amaretto Florentines are laced with liqueur and laden with sliced almonds. The beautiful airy look comes from spreading spoonfuls of the dough in thin layers.

amaretto florentines

Line a baking sheet with parchment paper; set aside.

In a heavy medium saucepan, combine butter, sugar, and whipping cream over medium-high heat. Stirring frequently, bring mixture to a boil. Remove from heat; cool to room temperature. Add almonds, flour, amaretto, and almond extract; stir until well blended.

Drop teaspoonfuls of dough 4 inches apart onto prepared baking sheet. Spread dough with back of spoon to form a thin layer. Bake at 350° for 5 to 7 minutes or until edges are lightly browned. Leaving cookies on parchment paper, remove paper from pan. Cool cookies 3 minutes; transfer to a wire rack to cool completely. Store in single layers between sheets of waxed paper.

YIELD: about 3$\frac{1}{2}$ dozen cookies

3 tablespoons butter

$\frac{1}{3}$ cup sugar

2 tablespoons whipping cream

1 cup sliced almonds

$\frac{1}{4}$ cup all-purpose flour

2 tablespoons amaretto

$\frac{1}{2}$ teaspoon almond extract

Based on the classic butter cookie, our sandy French Sablés (on left in photo) are flavored with lemon zest and toasted ground almonds. Walnut Crisps are light and crunchy fare that combine the flavors of walnuts and cinnamon.

French sablés

In a large bowl, cream butter and sugars until fluffy. Add egg, egg yolk, and lemon zest; beat until smooth. In a medium bowl, combine flour and ground almonds. Add dry ingredients to creamed mixture; stir until a soft dough forms. Divide dough in half. Wrap in plastic wrap and chill 1 hour or until firm enough to handle.

On a lightly floured surface, roll out $1/2$ of dough at a time to $1/4$-inch thickness. Use a 3-inch-diameter fluted-edge cookie cutter to cut out cookies. Place on a greased baking sheet. Score tops with tip of a sharp knife; brush with beaten egg white. Bake at 350° for 10 to 12 minutes or until bottoms are lightly browned. Transfer cookies to a wire rack to cool.

YIELD: about 3 dozen cookies

$3/4$ cup butter or margarine, softened
$1/2$ cup granulated sugar
$1/4$ cup confectioners sugar
1 egg
1 egg, separated
2 teaspoons grated lemon zest
$2^{1}/_{2}$ cups all-purpose flour
$2/3$ cup slivered almonds, toasted and finely ground

walnut crisps

In a large bowl, cream butter and $1/2$ cup sugar until fluffy. Add egg and vanilla; beat until smooth. In a small bowl, combine flour, baking powder, and cinnamon. Add dry ingredients to creamed mixture; stir until a soft dough forms. Stir in walnuts.

Shape dough into 1-inch balls and roll in sugar. Place balls 2 inches apart on an ungreased baking sheet; flatten with bottom of a glass that has been greased and dipped in sugar. Bake at 375° for 6 to 8 minutes or until bottoms are lightly browned. Transfer cookies to a wire rack to cool. Store in a cookie tin.

YIELD: about 4 dozen cookies

$1/2$ cup butter or margarine, softened
$1/2$ cup sugar
1 egg
1 teaspoon vanilla extract
$1^{1}/_{4}$ cups all-purpose flour
1 teaspoon baking powder
$1/2$ teaspoon ground cinnamon
1 cup finely chopped walnuts
Sugar

Named for a city in British Columbia where they originated in the 1950s, sumptuous three-layer Nanaimo Bars have inspired more than 100 variations. Ours features a chocolaty coconut-walnut crust, a buttercream filling, and a drizzled chocolate topping.

Nanaimo bars

For filling, whisk egg yolks in a small bowl until well blended. In a heavy small saucepan, combine sugar and water. Bring to a boil over medium-high heat. Remove from heat. Whisk a small amount of hot sugar mixture into egg yolks. Stirring constantly, return egg yolk mixture to saucepan and bring to a boil over medium heat; reduce heat to low. Stirring constantly, cook 2 minutes. Remove from heat. Stir in extracts. Pour into a small bowl; chill. In a medium bowl, cream butter until fluffy. Add chilled egg mixture; beat until smooth. Set aside.

For crust, melt butter in a heavy medium saucepan over low heat. Add chocolate chips, stirring until melted. Remove from heat. Stir in coconut, cracker crumbs, and walnuts. Press mixture into bottom of a greased 9-inch square baking pan. Chill in pan 5 minutes to allow chocolate to harden. Spread filling over crust; cover and chill 20 minutes. Cut into 1½-inch squares.

For topping, melt chocolate chips and shortening in a heavy small saucepan over low heat. Remove from heat. Drizzle chocolate over bars. Chill until chocolate hardens. Store in refrigerator.

YIELD: about 3 dozen bars

FILLING

- 2 egg yolks
- ⅓ cup sugar
- 2 tablespoons water
- ½ teaspoon vanilla extract
- ½ teaspoon orange extract
- ½ cup butter, softened

CRUST

- ½ cup butter or margarine
- ½ cup semisweet chocolate chips
- 1 cup sweetened shredded coconut
- 1 cup graham cracker crumbs
- 1 cup finely chopped walnuts

TOPPING

- ½ cup semisweet chocolate chips
- 2 teaspoons vegetable shortening

A hint of liquor gives both these cookies satisfying flavor. The tender Scotchies feature Scotch whiskey, pecans, and finely chopped butterscotch chips. The Chocolate-Brandy Drops have a similar texture but use brandy, pecans, and processed chocolate chips.

scotchies

In a large bowl, cream butter and 1 cup confectioners sugar until fluffy. Add flour and whiskey, stirring until a soft dough forms. Process butterscotch chips in a food processor until finely chopped. Stir chopped chips and pecans into dough.

Shape tablespoonfuls of dough into crescent shapes and place on a greased baking sheet. Bake at 350° for 12 to 15 minutes or until bottoms are lightly browned. Coat warm cookies with confectioners sugar. Transfer cookies to a wire rack with waxed paper underneath to cool. Coat with confectioners sugar again.

YIELD: about 4$\frac{1}{2}$ dozen cookies

1 cup butter or margarine, softened

1 cup confectioners sugar

2$\frac{1}{2}$ cups all-purpose flour

6 tablespoons Scotch whiskey

$\frac{1}{2}$ cup butterscotch chips, chilled

1 cup finely chopped pecans

Confectioners sugar

chocolate-brandy drops

In a large bowl, cream butter and sugars until fluffy. Process chocolate chips in a food processor until finely chopped. Add chocolate and remaining ingredients to creamed mixture, stirring until a soft dough forms.

Drop teaspoonfuls of dough 2 inches apart onto a greased baking sheet. Bake at 350° for 12 to 15 minutes or until bottoms are lightly browned. Transfer cookies to a wire rack to cool.

YIELD: about 3 dozen cookies

1 cup butter or margarine, softened

1 cup confectioners sugar

$\frac{1}{2}$ cup granulated sugar

1 cup semisweet chocolate chips, chilled

3 cups all-purpose flour

6 tablespoons brandy

1 cup finely chopped pecans

Coffee is the magic ingredient in these cookies and in their luscious icing. Perfect for an after-dinner sweet, the dough also contains orange zest, orange and vanilla extracts, and cinnamon.

orange-cappuccino cookies

For cookies, dissolve instant coffee in hot water in a small bowl; set aside. In a large bowl, cream butter and sugars until fluffy. Add egg, orange zest, extracts, and coffee mixture; beat until smooth. In a small bowl, combine flour, baking powder, cinnamon, and salt. Add dry ingredients to creamed mixture; stir until a soft dough forms. Wrap dough in plastic wrap and chill 2 hours or until firm enough to handle.

Shape dough into 1-inch balls and place 2 inches apart on a lightly greased baking sheet. Slightly flatten balls to $1^3/_4$-inch diameter with greased bottom of a glass. Bake at 375° for 7 to 9 minutes or until bottoms are lightly browned. Transfer cookies to a wire rack with waxed paper underneath to cool.

For icing, dissolve instant coffee in hot water in a medium bowl. Add confectioners sugar; stir until smooth. Ice cookies. Allow icing to harden. Store in single layers between sheets of waxed paper.

YIELD: about 4 dozen cookies

COOKIES

- 1 tablespoon instant coffee granules
- 1 tablespoon hot water
- $^1/_2$ cup butter or margarine, softened
- $^3/_4$ cup granulated sugar
- $^1/_4$ cup firmly packed brown sugar
- 1 egg
- 1 teaspoon orange zest
- $^1/_2$ teaspoon orange extract
- $^1/_2$ teaspoon vanilla extract
- 2 cups all-purpose flour
- 1 teaspoon baking powder
- $^1/_2$ teaspoon ground cinnamon
- $^1/_8$ teaspoon salt

ICING

- $3^1/_2$ teaspoons instant coffee granules
- $2^1/_2$ tablespoons hot water
- 2 cups confectioners sugar

In Italy, the term biscotti refers to any type of cookie, but Americans use the word to distinguish long, hard, twice-baked cookies designed for dunking in coffee, tea, or wine. This variation will fill your home with the citrusy aroma of lemon and licorice.

anise seed biscotti

Grease and flour a baking sheet; set aside.

In a large bowl, cream butter and sugar until fluffy. Add eggs, lemon zest, and lemon extract; beat until smooth. In a medium bowl, combine flour, anise seed, baking powder, baking soda, and salt. Add dry ingredients to creamed mixture; stir until a soft dough forms.

Divide dough in half. Spacing 3 inches apart on prepared baking sheet, shape each piece of dough into a $2^{1}/_{2}$ x 10-inch loaf, flouring hands as necessary. Bake at 375° for 23 to 27 minutes or until loaves are lightly browned; cool 10 minutes on baking sheet.

Cut loaves diagonally into $^{1}/_{2}$-inch-thick slices. Place slices flat on an ungreased baking sheet. Bake at 375° for 5 to 7 minutes; turn slices over and bake 5 to 7 more minutes or until lightly browned. Transfer cookies to a wire rack to cool. Store in a cookie tin.

YIELD: about $2^{1}/_{2}$ dozen cookies

- $^{1}/_{2}$ cup butter or margarine, softened
- 1 cup sugar
- 3 eggs
- 1 tablespoon lemon zest
- 1 teaspoon lemon extract
- 3 cups all-purpose flour
- 1 tablespoon anise seed
- 1 teaspoon baking powder
- $^{1}/_{2}$ teaspoon baking soda
- $^{1}/_{8}$ teaspoon salt

Decorated with piped drops of delicate lemon icing, traditional German Lebkuchen cookies combine the tastes of honey, cocoa, and spices. We used a scalloped heart-shaped cookie cutter to give ours a pretty look.

German lebkuchen

For cookies, cream butter, honey, and sugar in a large bowl. Add egg, lemon zest, and vanilla; beat until smooth. In a medium bowl, combine flour, cocoa, cinnamon, allspice, cloves, ginger, cardamom, baking powder, and baking soda. Add dry ingredients to creamed mixture; stir until a soft dough forms. Divide dough into fourths. Wrap in plastic wrap and chill overnight or until firm enough to handle.

On a lightly floured surface, roll out $1/4$ of dough at a time to $1/4$-inch thickness. Use a 4-inch-wide heart-shaped fluted-edge cookie cutter to cut out cookies. Place on a lightly greased baking sheet. Bake at 350° for 8 to 10 minutes or until edges are lightly browned. Transfer cookies to a wire rack with waxed paper underneath to cool.

For icing, combine all ingredients in a small bowl; stir until smooth. Spoon icing into a decorating bag fitted with a very small round tip. Pipe desired decorations onto cookies. Allow icing to harden.

YIELD: about 3 dozen cookies

COOKIES

$1^1/2$ cups butter, softened

$3/4$ cup honey

$3/4$ cup sugar

1 egg

2 tablespoons grated lemon zest

1 teaspoon vanilla extract

4 cups all-purpose flour

2 tablespoons cocoa

2 teaspoons ground cinnamon

1 teaspoon ground allspice

1 teaspoon ground cloves

1 teaspoon ground ginger

$1/4$ teaspoon ground cardamom

$1/4$ teaspoon baking powder

$1/4$ teaspoon baking soda

ICING

$1^1/4$ cups confectioners sugar

1 tablespoon lemon juice

1 tablespoon water

SPECIAL OCCASIONS

Any time there's a reason to celebrate, one of the first things
we do is plan something good to eat. Cookies are a favorite choice,
offering an unlimited range of rich tastes and textures.

Zesty lemon flavor and softly tinted yellow icing make these buttery cookies
perfect for little duck shapes to serve at a baby shower. The expectant mom's
gifts won't be the only things making guests say, "Oh, how cute!"

lemon cookies

For cookies, cream butter, sugar, and lemon peel in a large bowl until
fluffy. Stir in flour; knead dough until a soft ball forms. Wrap in plastic
wrap and chill 30 minutes.

On a lightly floured surface, roll out dough to ¼-inch thickness. Use
a duck-shaped cookie cutter to cut out cookies. Place cookies on
a greased baking sheet. Bake at 300° for 20 to 25 minutes or until
bottoms are lightly browned. Transfer cookies to a wire rack with
waxed paper underneath.

For icing, combine confectioners sugar and milk in a medium bowl;
tint yellow. Pour icing over cookies, smoothing with a spatula.
Decorate with candies for eyes. Allow icing to harden.

YIELD: about 5 dozen cookies

COOKIES

- 1 cup butter or margarine, softened
- ½ cup granulated sugar
- 1 teaspoon grated dried lemon peel
- 2½ cups all-purpose flour

ICING

- 2¼ cups confectioners sugar
- 5 tablespoons milk
- Yellow paste food coloring
- Small white candy decorations for eyes

For parties that are swirling with excitement, let these cookies help reflect the mood.
The easy-to-make cookies have all the good, spicy flavor of Grandma's traditional version.

date pinwheels

In a large bowl, cream butter, brown sugar, egg, and vanilla. In a separate bowl, combine flour, baking soda, salt, $1/2$ teaspoon cinnamon, and nutmeg. Stir flour mixture into creamed mixture. Wrap in plastic wrap and chill 2 hours.

In a saucepan, combine dates, water, granulated sugar, and remaining $1/4$ teaspoon cinnamon. Cook, stirring constantly, over low heat until mixture thickens; cool.

Divide dough into thirds. Roll out $1/3$ of dough at a time into an 8 x 10-inch x $1/4$-inch-thick rectangle. Spread $1/3$ of date mixture over each rectangle. Starting with one long end, roll up dough. Cut into $1/2$-inch-thick slices. Place on a lightly greased baking sheet. Bake at 350° for 14 to 16 minutes or until lightly browned. Transfer cookies to a wire rack to cool.

YIELD: about 5 dozen cookies

$1/2$ cup butter or margarine, softened

1 cup firmly packed brown sugar

1 egg

$1 1/2$ teaspoons vanilla extract

2 cups all-purpose flour

$1/2$ teaspoon baking soda

$1/2$ teaspoon salt

$3/4$ teaspoon ground cinnamon, divided

$1/4$ teaspoon ground nutmeg

1 package (8 ounces) chopped dates

$1/2$ cup water

$1/4$ cup granulated sugar

Making new friends in the neighborhood will be a delicious pleasure when you reach out with a plateful of Raspberry Thumbprint Cookies. Enriched with chocolate mini chips, the cookies have a scrumptious topping of raspberry preserves.

raspberry thumbprint cookies

In a medium bowl, cream butter, sugars, vanilla, and salt until light and fluffy. Blend in flour and milk. Stir in chocolate chips.

Shape dough into 1-inch balls and place 1 inch apart on an ungreased baking sheet. Use thumb or the back of a small, round measuring spoon to make a small indentation in the top of each ball. Spoon a small amount of raspberry preserves into each indentation. Bake at 375° for 10 to 12 minutes. Transfer cookies to a wire rack to cool.

YIELD: about 3 dozen cookies

$1/2$ cup butter or margarine, softened

$1/4$ cup firmly packed brown sugar

$1/4$ cup granulated sugar

1 teaspoon vanilla extract

$1/2$ teaspoon salt

$1^1/2$ cups all-purpose flour

2 tablespoons milk

$1/3$ cup semisweet chocolate mini chips

Raspberry preserves

These rich cookies offer old-fashioned goodness that will enhance any celebration. Their popular combination of chocolate, peanut butter, and butterscotch chips guarantees satisfaction.

triple chip cookies

In a medium bowl, cream butter and sugars. Beat in eggs and vanilla. In a small bowl, combine flour, baking soda, baking powder, and salt; gradually add to creamed mixture. Stir in chips.

Drop heaping teaspoonfuls of dough 2 inches apart onto a greased baking sheet. Bake at 350° for 10 to 12 minutes or until bottoms are lightly browned. Transfer cookies to a wire rack to cool.

YIELD: about 6 dozen cookies

1 cup butter or margarine, softened

$1^1/_2$ cups firmly packed brown sugar

$^1/_2$ cup granulated sugar

2 eggs

2 teaspoons vanilla extract

2 cups all-purpose flour

1 teaspoon baking soda

$^1/_2$ teaspoon baking powder

$^1/_2$ teaspoon salt

$1^1/_2$ cups semisweet chocolate chips

1 cup peanut butter chips

$^3/_4$ cup butterscotch chips

Yummy almond bites rolled in confectioners sugar, Sandies are a traditional treat for occasions that call for the richest, best foods available. Traced to Medieval times, the cookies have been known since the 1950s as Mexican or Greek Wedding Cookies.

sandies

In a large bowl, cream butter and $1/2$ cup confectioners sugar until fluffy. Stir in extracts. In a medium bowl, combine flour and salt. Add dry ingredients to creamed mixture; stir until a soft dough forms. Stir in almonds.

Shape dough into 1-inch balls and place 2 inches apart on an ungreased baking sheet. Bake at 350° for 12 to 15 minutes or until bottoms are lightly browned. Roll warm cookies in remaining $1 1/2$ cups confectioners sugar. Transfer cookies to a wire rack with waxed paper underneath to cool. Roll in confectioners sugar again.

YIELD: about $4 1/2$ dozen cookies

- 1 cup butter or margarine, softened
- 2 cups confectioners sugar, divided
- 1 teaspoon almond extract
- $1/2$ teaspoon vanilla extract
- $2 1/4$ cups all-purpose flour
- $1/4$ teaspoon salt
- 1 cup slivered almonds, toasted and coarsely ground

To help a couple celebrate their new home, show up at the housewarming with a pretty dish of Cashew Dreams. The nutty shortbread cookies are easy to make with just a few ingredients.

cashew dreams

For cookies, cream butter, sugar, and vanilla in a medium bowl until fluffy. Add flour; stir until a soft dough forms. Stir in $1\frac{1}{4}$ cups chopped cashews.

Shape dough into 1-inch balls and place 2 inches apart on a greased baking sheet. Slightly flatten balls with fingers. Bake at 325° for 8 to 10 minutes or until bottoms are lightly browned. Transfer cookies to a wire rack to cool.

For icing, combine confectioners sugar, $1\frac{1}{2}$ tablespoons milk, and vanilla in a small bowl; stir until smooth, adding additional milk as necessary, $\frac{1}{2}$ teaspoon at a time, to spread easily. Ice cookies; sprinkle tops with remaining $\frac{1}{4}$ cup chopped cashews. Allow icing to harden.

YIELD: about 4 dozen cookies

COOKIES

- 1 cup butter or margarine, softened
- 6 tablespoons sugar
- 1 teaspoon vanilla extract
- 2 cups all-purpose flour
- $1\frac{1}{2}$ cups coarsely chopped lightly salted cashews, divided

ICING

- $1\frac{1}{4}$ cups confectioners sugar
- $1\frac{1}{2}$ to 2 tablespoons milk
- $\frac{1}{2}$ teaspoon vanilla extract

Sharing these Afternoon Tea Cakes and a refreshing pot of tea with good friends is a delicious way to spend an afternoon. Touched with a hint of orange, the cakes are simply dreamy!

afternoon tea cakes

In a medium bowl, cream butter and sugar until fluffy. Add egg and extracts; beat until smooth. In a small bowl, combine flour, baking powder, and salt. Add dry ingredients to creamed mixture; stir until a soft dough forms. Divide dough into fourths. Wrap in plastic wrap and chill 1 to 2 hours.

On a lightly floured surface, roll out $1/4$ of dough at a time to $1/8$-inch thickness. Use a $2^1/2$-inch round fluted-edge cookie cutter to cut out cookies. Place 2 inches apart on a lightly greased baking sheet. Bake at 400° for 6 to 8 minutes or until edges are lightly browned. Transfer cookies to a wire rack to cool.

YIELD: about $3^1/2$ dozen cookies

$1/2$ cup butter or margarine, softened
1 cup sugar
1 egg
1 teaspoon vanilla extract
$1/4$ teaspoon orange extract
2 cups all-purpose flour
2 teaspoons baking powder
$1/2$ teaspoon salt

To spice up an ice cream party, serve each scoop on a moist Gingerbread Cutout and smother with caramel sauce. We cut our gingerbread in simple circles, but lots of fun shapes are possible when you use cookie cutters.

gingerbread cutouts

Line a 15 x 10 x 1-inch jellyroll pan with waxed paper; set aside.

In a large bowl, cream shortening, sugar, and egg. Blend in molasses and water. In a medium bowl, combine flour, baking soda, salt, ginger, cinnamon, and cloves; add to molasses mixture. Beat until smooth.

Pour into prepared pan. Bake at 325° for 30 to 35 minutes or until a toothpick inserted in center comes out clean. Cool in pan. Use a $3^{1}/_{2}$-inch round cookie cutter to cut out gingerbread. Serve with ice cream and caramel sauce.

YIELD: about 3 dozen cutouts

$^{1}/_{2}$ cup vegetable shortening
2 tablespoons sugar
1 egg
1 cup molasses
1 cup boiling water
$2^{1}/_{4}$ cups all-purpose flour
1 teaspoon baking soda
$^{1}/_{2}$ teaspoon salt
$1^{1}/_{2}$ teaspoons ground ginger
1 teaspoon ground cinnamon
$^{1}/_{2}$ teaspoon ground cloves
Ice cream and caramel sauce to serve

Kids love bright colors and fun shapes, and any snack can turn into a party with these tasty treats created using a cookie press. To bring on an extra round of giggles, explain that the cookie's name comes from the German word *spritzen*, which means "to squirt."

cream cheese spritz

In a large bowl, cream shortening and cream cheese. Gradually add sugar and mix well. Beat in egg yolk and vanilla. In a medium bowl, combine flour, salt, and cinnamon; gradually add to creamed mixture. Divide dough into as many portions as desired and tint each one a different color. Follow cookie press instructions to form cookies on an ungreased baking sheet. Bake at 350° for 12 to 15 minutes. Transfer cookies to a wire rack to cool.

YIELD: about 6 dozen cookies

1 cup vegetable shortening

1 package (3 ounces) cream cheese, softened

1 cup sugar

1 egg yolk

1 teaspoon vanilla extract

2 1/2 cups all-purpose flour

1/2 teaspoon salt

1/4 teaspoon ground cinnamon

Paste food colorings, if desired

Cut with a bell-shaped cookie cutter, these tender sugar cookies are elegant for serving at a wedding rehearsal dinner or formal reception. The cookies are beautifully topped with almond-flavored icing and silvery decorations.

wedding bells

For cookies, cream butter and sugars in a large bowl until fluffy. Add egg and almond extract; beat until smooth. In a medium bowl, combine flour, baking powder, and salt. Add dry ingredients to creamed mixture; stir until a soft dough forms. On a lightly floured surface, roll out dough to $1/4$-inch thickness. Use a 3 x 3-inch bell-shaped cookie cutter to cut out cookies. Place 2 inches apart on a greased baking sheet. Bake at 375° for 7 to 9 minutes or until bottoms are lightly browned. Transfer cookies to a wire rack with waxed paper underneath to cool.

For icing, combine water and corn syrup in a heavy medium saucepan. Add confectioners sugar and stir until well blended. Attach a candy thermometer to pan, making sure thermometer does not touch bottom of pan. Stirring constantly, cook over medium-low heat until icing reaches 100°. Remove from heat; stir in almond extract. Cool icing 5 minutes. Stirring icing occasionally, ice cookies. Decorate cookies with dragées before icing hardens. Allow icing to harden.

YIELD: about $4^1/2$ dozen cookies

COOKIES

- 1 cup butter or margarine, softened
- 1 cup granulated sugar
- $1/2$ cup confectioners sugar
- 1 egg
- 1 teaspoon almond extract
- $2^1/2$ cups all-purpose flour
- $1/2$ teaspoon baking powder
- $1/4$ teaspoon salt

ICING

- $1/4$ cup water
- 1 tablespoon light corn syrup
- 3 cups plus 3 tablespoons confectioners sugar
- $1/2$ teaspoon almond extract
  Silver dragées to decorate (Dragées are for decoration only; remove before eating cookies.)

Reminiscent of the crisp animal crackers that toddlers love to munch, these lightly sweetened Honey Grahams add a playful touch to the refreshments at a baby shower. People of all ages will love their nostalgic taste as well as their animal shapes.

honey grahams

Combine all ingredients in a large bowl; knead dough until a soft ball forms. Wrap in plastic wrap and chill 30 minutes.

On a lightly floured surface, roll out dough to $^1/_8$-inch thickness. Use desired animal-shaped cookie cutters to cut out dough. Place on an ungreased baking sheet. Bake at 425° for 3 to 5 minutes or until golden brown. Cool cookies on baking sheet (cookies will become crisp as they cool).

YIELD: about 3 dozen cookies

$1^1/_2$ cups whole-wheat graham flour

1 cup all-purpose flour

$^1/_2$ cup vegetable shortening

$^1/_3$ cup firmly packed brown sugar

$^1/_4$ cup honey

$^1/_4$ cup vegetable oil

3 tablespoons cold water

1 teaspoon baking soda

1 teaspoon ground cinnamon

$^1/_2$ teaspoon salt

For a creative treat at a children's party, surprise them with Artist's Palette Cookies. Simply use our pattern to cut out the cookie "palettes" and add splashes of colored icing for the "paint." Everyone will think these oatmeal-pecan cookies are truly masterpieces!

artist's palette cookies

For convenience, substitute tubes of ready-to-use decorating icing in red, blue, green, and yellow.

For cookies, process oats in a food processor until finely ground. In a large bowl, cream butter and sugar until fluffy. Add eggs and vanilla; beat until smooth. In a medium bowl, combine processed oats, flour, baking soda, and salt. Add dry ingredients to creamed mixture; stir until a soft dough forms. Stir in pecans. Divide dough in half. Wrap in plastic wrap and chill 1 hour.

On a lightly floured surface, roll out $1/2$ of dough at a time to $1/8$-inch thickness. Use pattern, page 142, and a sharp knife to cut out cookies. Place 1 inch apart on a greased baking sheet. Use a plastic drinking straw to cut a hole in each cookie. Bake at 350° for 6 to 8 minutes or until edges are lightly browned. Transfer cookies to a wire rack to cool.

For icing, combine confectioners sugar, milk, and vanilla in a medium bowl; stir until smooth. Place about 3 tablespoons of icing in each of 4 small bowls and tint red, blue, green, and yellow. Spoon each color of icing into a separate squeeze bottle or a small plastic bag with one corner snipped off. Decorate cookies with icing. Allow icing to harden.

YIELD: about 8 dozen cookies

COOKIES

$1^{1}/_{2}$ cups old-fashioned oats
1 cup butter or margarine, softened
$1^{1}/_{4}$ cups sugar
2 eggs
1 teaspoon vanilla extract
$2^{1}/_{4}$ cups all-purpose flour
1 teaspoon baking soda
$1/_{2}$ teaspoon salt
$3/_{4}$ cup chopped pecans, toasted and finely ground

ICING

2 cups confectioners sugar
3 tablespoons plus 1 teaspoon milk
$1/_{2}$ teaspoon vanilla extract
Red, blue, green, and yellow liquid food colorings and 4 small squeeze bottles with small tips

Poppy seeds bring delightful crunch and a slightly nutty taste to these pretty lemon-flavored cookies. The delicate flavor goes wonderfully with tea.

poppy seed cookies

In a large bowl, beat oil and sugar until well blended. Add eggs and extracts; beat until smooth. In a medium bowl, combine flour, poppy seed, baking powder, and salt. Add dry ingredients to sugar mixture; stir until a soft dough forms. Divide dough into fourths.

On a heavily floured surface, roll out $1/4$ of dough at a time to $1/4$-inch thickness. Use a floured 3-inch round flower-shaped cookie cutter to cut out cookies. Place on a greased baking sheet. Bake at 400° for 5 to 7 minutes or until edges are lightly browned. Transfer cookies to a wire rack to cool.

YIELD: about $4^1/_2$ dozen cookies

$3/4$	cup vegetable oil
1	cup sugar
3	eggs
2	teaspoons vanilla extract
1	teaspoon lemon extract
$3^1/_2$	cups all-purpose flour
$1/4$	cup poppy seed
1	teaspoon baking powder
$1/8$	teaspoon salt

KITCHEN TIPS

NOTE: *For additional tips, see Success With Cookies on page 7.*

MEASURING INGREDIENTS

Liquid measuring cups have a rim above the measuring line to keep liquid ingredients from spilling. Nested measuring cups are used to measure dry ingredients, butter, shortening, and peanut butter. Measuring spoons are used for measuring both dry and liquid ingredients.

To measure flour or granulated sugar: Spoon ingredient into nested measuring cup and level off with a knife. Do not pack down with spoon.

To measure confectioners sugar: Sift sugar, spoon lightly into nested measuring cup, and level off with a knife.

To measure brown sugar: Pack sugar into nested measuring cup and level off with a knife. Sugar should hold its shape when removed from cup.

To measure butter, shortening, or peanut butter: Pack ingredient firmly into nested measuring cup and level off with a knife.

To measure liquids: Use a liquid measuring cup placed on a flat surface. Pour ingredient into cup and check measuring line at eye level.

To measure honey or syrup: For a more accurate measurement, lightly spray measuring cup or spoon with cooking spray before measuring so the liquid will release easily from cup or spoon.

SOFTENING BUTTER OR MARGARINE

To soften butter, remove wrapper from butter and place on a microwave-safe plate. Microwave 1 stick 20 to 30 seconds at medium-low power (30%).

SOFTENING CREAM CHEESE

To soften cream cheese, remove wrapper from cream cheese and place on a microwave-safe plate. Microwave 1 to $1^1/_2$ minutes at medium power (50%) for an 8-ounce package or 30 to 45 seconds for a 3-ounce package.

WHIPPING CREAM

For greatest volume, chill a glass bowl, beaters, and cream until well chilled before whipping. In warm weather, place chilled bowl over ice while whipping cream.

TOASTING NUTS

To toast nuts, spread nuts on an ungreased baking sheet. Stirring occasionally, bake 8 to 10 minutes in a preheated 350-degree oven until nuts are slightly darker in color.

PREPARING CITRUS FRUIT ZEST

To remove outer portion of peel (colored part) from citrus fruits, use a fine grater or fruit zester, being careful not to cut into the bitter white portion. Zest is also referred to as grated peel.

BEATING EGG WHITES

For greatest volume, beat egg whites at room temperature in a clean, dry metal or glass bowl.

TO BLANCH ALMONDS

Place 1 cup water in a 1-quart bowl or casserole; cover. Microwave on high power (100%) 3 minutes. Add 1 cup whole shelled almonds. Microwave on high power (100%) 1 minute uncovered; drain and remove peel from nuts. Dry on paper towels.

USING CHOCOLATE

Chocolate is best stored in a cool, dry place. Since it has a high content of cocoa butter, chocolate may develop a grey film, or "bloom," when temperatures change. This grey film does not affect the taste.

When melting chocolate, a low temperature is important to prevent overheating and scorching that will affect flavor and texture.

The following are methods for melting chocolate:

- Chocolate can be melted in a heavy saucepan over low heat, stirring constantly until melted.

- Melting chocolate in a double boiler over hot, not boiling, water is a good method to prevent chocolate from overheating.

- Using a microwave to melt chocolate is fast and convenient. To microwave chocolate, place in a microwave-safe container and microwave on medium-high power (80%) 1 minute; stir with a dry spoon. Continue to microwave 15 seconds at a time, stirring chocolate after each interval until smooth. Frequent stirring is important, as the chocolate will appear not to be melting, but will be soft when stirred. A shiny appearance is another sign that chocolate is melting.

MAKING PATTERNS FOR COOKIES

Place a piece of white paper over pattern (for a more durable pattern, use acetate, a thin plastic used for stenciling that is available at craft stores). Use a permanent felt-tip pen with fine point to trace pattern; cut out pattern. Place pattern on rolled-out dough and use a small sharp knife to cut out cookies. (Note: If dough is sticky, dip knife frequently into flour while cutting out cookies.)

CUTTING DIAMOND-SHAPED BARS

To cut 1³/₄-inch-wide x 3-inch-long diamond-shaped pieces, start at 1 short edge of pan and make 1¹/₂-inch-wide cuts (*Fig. 1*).

Fig. 1 1¹/₂"

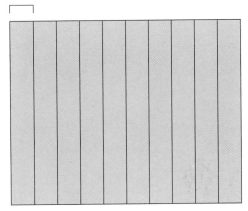

Make a diagonal cut from lower left corner to upper right corner (shown by heavy black line). Make 1¹/₂-inch-wide cuts on each side of first diagonal cut (*Fig. 2*).

Fig. 2

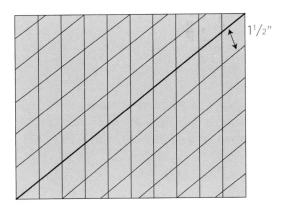

1¹/₂"

patterns

United States Maps
*recipe on page 49,
picture on page 48*

**Pumpkin
Cookie Pops**
*recipe on
page 68,
picture on
page 69*

Springtime Bunnies
*recipe on page 60,
picture on page 61*

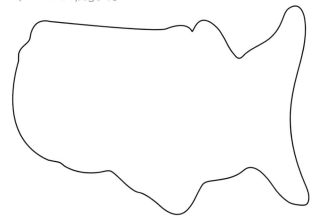

Ghost Cookies
recipe on page 67,
picture on page 66

Santa Cookies
recipe on page 72,
picture on page 73

Round Ornament Cookies
recipe on page 76, picture on page 77

Artist's Palette Cookies
recipe on page 135, picture on page 134

Spiced Christmas Stars
recipe on page 84, picture on page 85

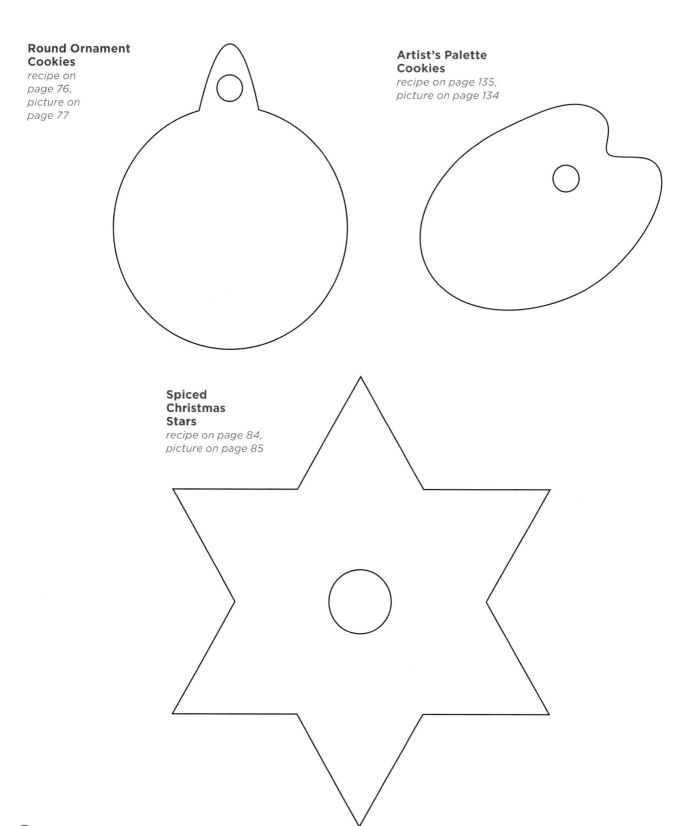

metric equivalents

The recipes that appear in this cookbook use the standard United States method for measuring liquid and dry or solid ingredients (teaspoons, tablespoons, and cups). The information on this chart is provided to help cooks outside the U.S. successfully use these recipes. All equivalents are approximate.

METRIC EQUIVALENTS FOR DIFFERENT TYPES OF INGREDIENTS

A standard cup measure of a dry or solid ingredient will vary in weight depending on the type of ingredient. A standard cup of liquid is the same volume for any type of liquid. Use the following chart when converting standard cup measures to grams (weight) or milliliters (volume).

Standard Cup	Fine Powder (ex. flour)	Grain (ex. rice)	Granular (ex. sugar)	Liquid Solids (ex. butter)	Liquid (ex. milk)
1	140 g	150 g	190 g	200 g	240 ml
¾	105 g	113 g	143 g	150 g	180 ml
⅔	93 g	100 g	125 g	133 g	160 ml
½	70 g	75 g	95 g	100 g	120 ml
⅓	47 g	50 g	63 g	67 g	80 ml
¼	35 g	38 g	48 g	50 g	60 ml
⅛	18 g	19 g	24 g	25 g	30 ml

USEFUL EQUIVALENTS FOR LIQUID INGREDIENTS BY VOLUME

¼ tsp						=	1 ml
½ tsp						=	2 ml
1 tsp						=	5 ml
3 tsp	=	1 tbls			½ fl oz	=	15 ml
		2 tbls	=	⅛ cup	= 1 fl oz	=	30 ml
		4 tbls	=	¼ cup	= 2 fl oz	=	60 ml
		5 ⅓ tbls	=	⅓ cup	= 3 fl oz	=	80 ml
		8 tbls	=	½ cup	= 4 fl oz	=	120 ml
		10 ⅔ tbls	=	⅔ cup	= 5 fl oz	=	160 ml
		12 tbls	=	¾ cup	= 6 fl oz	=	180 ml
		16 tbls	=	1 cup	= 8 fl oz	=	240 ml
1 pt	=	2 cups	=		16 fl oz	=	480 ml
1 qt	=	4 cups	=		32 fl oz	=	960 ml
			=		33 fl oz	=	1000 ml = 1 liter

USEFUL EQUIVALENTS FOR DRY INGREDIENTS BY WEIGHT
(To convert ounces to grams, multiply the number of ounces by 30.)

1 oz	=	1/16 lb	=	30 g
4 oz	=	¼ lb	=	120 g
8 oz	=	½ lb	=	240 g
12 oz	=	¾ lb	=	360 g
16 oz	=	1 lb	=	480 g

USEFUL EQUIVALENTS FOR LENGTH
(To convert inches to centimeters, multiply the number of inches by 2.5.)

1 in					=	2.5 cm	
6 in	=	½ ft			=	15 cm	
12 in	=	1 ft			=	30 cm	
36 in	=	3 ft	=	1 yd	=	90 cm	
40 in					=	100 cm	= 1 m

USEFUL EQUIVALENTS FOR COOKING/OVEN TEMPERATURES

	Fahrenheit	Celsius	Gas Mark
Freeze Water	32° F	0° C	
Room Temperature	68° F	20° C	
Boil Water	212° F	100° C	
Bake	325° F	160° C	3
	350° F	180° C	4
	375° F	190° C	5
	400° F	200° C	6
	425° F	220° C	7
	450° F	230° C	8
Broil			Grill

recipe index